EYEWITNESS TRAVELGUIDE TO
Buenos Aires

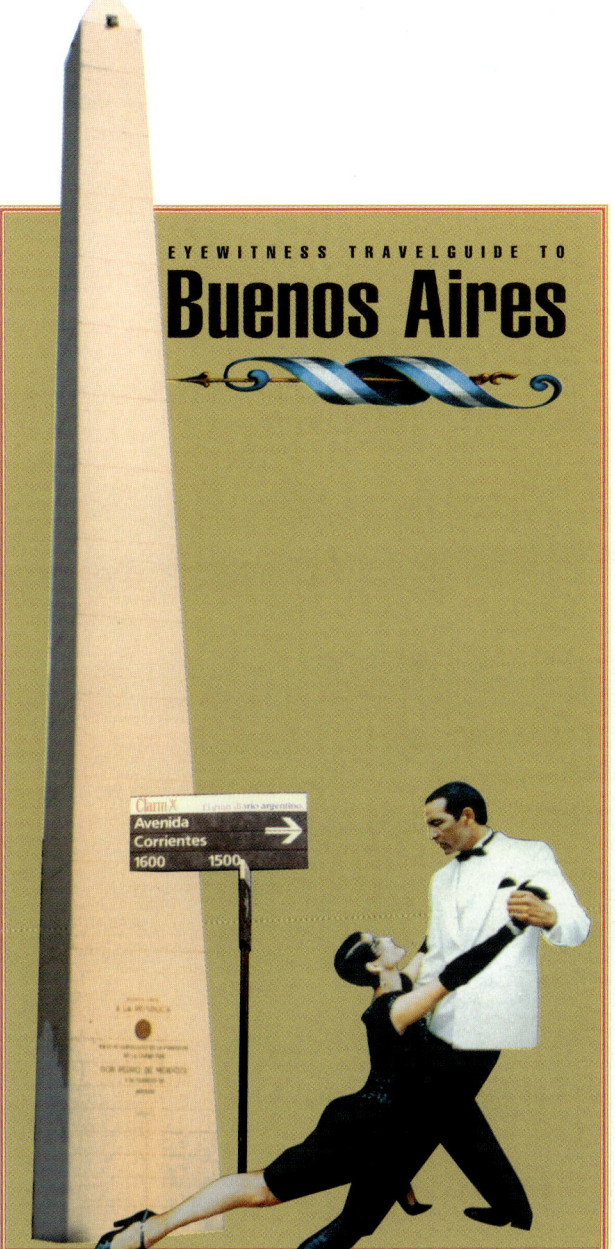

This book is a Publication of:

POSTERS AND BOOKS
Luis Saenz Peña 235 - 1ºpiso -
Tel./fax:4371-7690

Author:
Daniel Santoro

Staff:
Design: *Marcelo Rolla -
Daniel Santoro - Liliana Cascales.*
Drawings and Photos: *Daniel Santoro.*
Text: *Liliana Cascales -
Daniel Santoro*
Translator: *Victoria Rodil - María Gloria Municoy*

ISBN: 987-43-1484-2

No part of this publication may be reproduced, stored in a retrival system or transmitted in any form or by any means electronic, mechanical, photocopying, without the prior permission of the publisher.

*Preimpresión: SIGNOS
Uruguay 183*

2º Edition, year 2000

Buenos Aires **2000**

Auspicia:
*Secretaría de Turismo
del Gobierno de la Ciudad
de Buenos Aires.*

EYEWITNESS TRAVELGUIDE TO
Buenos Aires

Contents

5 Useful Information

History of the City of Buenos Aires **7**

8 Map of the city

Tours around Buenos Aires **10**

13 Plaza de Mayo and surrounding area

South of the Cathedral **25**

29 San Telmo

La Boca **37**

43 Puerto Madero

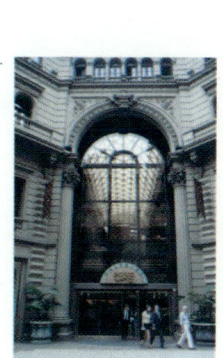

Retiro - San Martin Square **49**

57 Retiro - Alvear Avenue

Recoleta area **61**

73 Palermo

Barrio Norte **77**

81 Corrientes Avenue

Lavalle Square **87**

93 Congress Square

Abasto **98**

99 Tango Music

Beef **102**

103 Theaters, tango shows, museums, hotels

gastronomic guide **105**

107 Mate

Eyewitness Travelguide to Buenos Aires

AIRLINES

- Tel: 4374-0909
- Av. Santa Fe 1558 Piso 5°. Tel 4312-5573
- Bouchard 547 Tel 4340.-7777
- Av. Santa Fe 840 Tel 4311-4115
- Paraguay 610 Tel 4317-4700
- Esmeralda 1111 28° Tel: 4310-9999
- Av. Santa Fe 881 Tel 4318-1111
- Av. L.N. Alem 1134 Tel 4317-3600
- C. Pellegrini 1163 Tel:4322-2731
- Córdoba 650 Tel 4320-6600
- Av. Córdoba 656 Tel: 4322-3632
- Sarmiento 552 Tel: 4327-2244
- C. Pellegrini 675 Tel: 4327-22241

- Suipacha 1065 Tel 4311-3010
- C. Pellegrini 1163 Tel 4327-2739
- Tel 4312-2660
- Florida 868 - 13° E Tel 4313-5883
- Florida 954 Tel. 4316-2200
- M.T. de Alvear 636 Tel: 4319-0600
- Tel 4326-5272
- C. Pellegrini 1075 Tel:4819-5272
- Suipacha 1111 - 14° Tel 4313-4698
- Florida 1 Tel 4342-4420
- Av. Santa Fe 846 Tel: 4319-0000
- Av. Madero 900 Tel: 4316-07577
- Pasaje Carabelas 344 Tel 4329-9200
- Av. Santa Fe 784 Tel 4312-8520

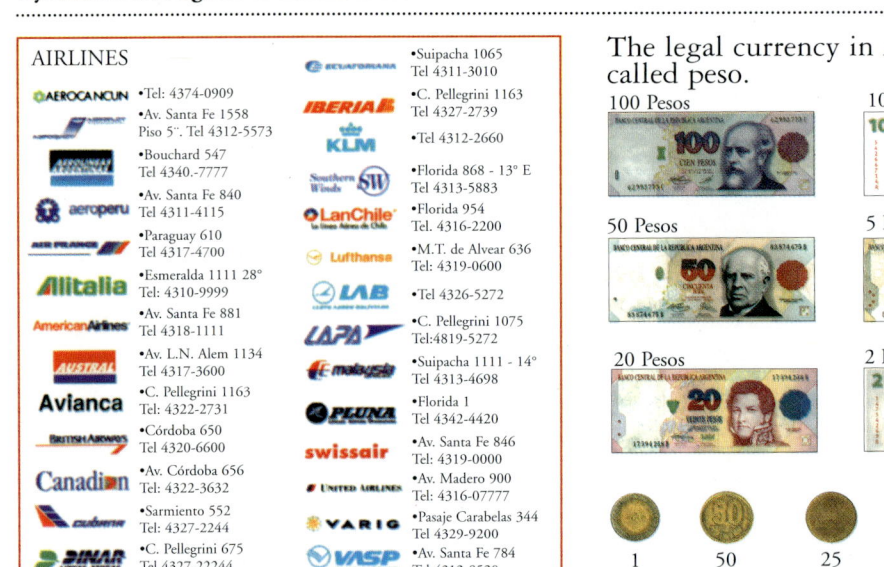

The legal currency in Argentina is called peso.

100 Pesos | 10 Pesos
50 Pesos | 5 Pesos
20 Pesos | 2 Pesos

1 Peso | 50 Centavos | 25 Centavos | 10 Centavos | 5 Centavos

4

Eyewitness Travelguide to Buenos Aires

PUBLIC HOLIDAYS
January 1: New Year
May 1: Labor Day
May 25: May Revolution
June 20: Flag Day
July 9: Independence Day
August 17: Anniversary of General San Martin's death
October 12: Columbus Day
December 25: Christmas

Taxis: They are black and yellow in color and they are easily found on the city's main streets. You may hail a taxi on any corner but it is much safer to call one on the phone through radiotaxi services. The minimum fare is $ 1.12 and the passenger should pay the amount on the fare meter. A trip from Palermo to La Boca should not be more expensive than $ 6. Tipping is not required.

Bus (colectivo): There are more than 150 bus lines in the city and the buses are easily seen on streets and avenues. The minimum fare for a trip within the city limits is $0.65 and the maximum fare is $ 0.70. Buses are furnished with automatic ticket machines that only accept coins.

Banks are open Monday through Friday from 10 AM to 3 PM. Shops are usually open from 9 AM to 8 PM. Shopping malls are open till 10 PM.

Tipping in restaurants and bars usually amounts to 10 % of the bill, though it will not be included in the bill.

Pay telephones may take either coins or calling cards, which may be found out by reading the message on the screen before using the phone.

SUBWAY LINES

Five subway lines and one Pre-Metro line run across most tourist-attractive areas in the city and the service is quite good and inexpensive ($ 0.50 and 0.25). The fare is paid through tokens, which may be purchased in any station. The following are the names and areas covered by each line:
Line A: It runs under Av de Mayo and Av. Rivadavia. It goes from Plaza de Mayo to Primera Junta and it has a stop at Congress Square.
Line B: It runs under Av. Corrientes. It goes from Leandro N. Alem station (behind the Argentina Postal Service Building) to Chacarita station. It stops at the Abasto market (Carlos Gardel station).
Line C: It runs under Av. 9 de Julio and other streets. It goes from Constitución station to Retiro station. You may change in Diagonal Norte station for the rest of the lines. It has a stop at San Martín Square.
Line D: It goes from the Cathedral in Plaza de Mayo to José Hernández station in Barrancas de Belgrano quarter. On its way to Barrio Norte, it stops at Callao station, Agüero station, Facultad de Medicina station (under the Medicine College of the University of Buenos Aires) and Palermo station. After that, it runs under Cabildo Avenue.
Line E: It runs under Av. San Juan and it goes form Plaza de Mayo to Virreyes station, where you may change for the Pre-Metro line.
Pre-Metro: It goes form Virreyes station to a theme park called Parque de la Ciudad. The fare is $ 0.25 for those who take it on Virreyes station, but it is free for those who are changing from Line E.

5

Eyewitness Travelguide to Buenos Aires

BREVE HISTORIA DE LA CIUDAD DE BUENOS AIRES.
Brief History of the City of Buenos Aires

PRIMERA FUNDACION: FIRST FOUNDATION

When facing the need to stop the Portuguese forces' advance, Carlos I, king of Spain, sent commander Pedro de Mendoza to establish a stone fort somewhere in the Río de la Plata area. This fort would serve as the origin for a new city.

In 1536, Pedro de Mendoza arrived in the Rio de la Plata banks with around 2,000 men and he found the right place to establish his fort on a high hill by the rivulet's outlet. He had some thatch-roofed mud huts built on a compact earth slope where we can find Lezama Park today. In the beginning, good relationships with Native Americans allowed him to exchange low-value articles for food and other necessities. However, it was not long before this harmony came to an end and famine struck, which caused the population not only to decrease seriously due to confrontations but also to witness awful cannibalism scenes.
Second Foundation: In 1580, a new expedition departed from

This is a picture by Santiago Carbonell where we can see the scene of the foundation of Buenos Aires in front of the tree of justice, where Plaza de Mayo stands today.

SEGUNDA FUNDACION.

Paraguay. This time it was Juan de Garay who founded the base for the second time. He gave this settlement the name of "Ciudad de la Santísima Trinidad y Puerto de Santa María de los Buenos Ayres". The site he chose was two kilometers north of the first settlement and there he planted the tree of justice as a symbol for the generations to come.

As ordered under the Laws of the Indies, town planners used a checkerboard plan for the layout of the town. The plan featured a Plaza Mayor or central square, 15 blocks from North to South and 9 blocks from East to West. The only opening in the checkerboard was the Plaza Mayor (currently Plaza de Mayo), where enough space was left for a fortress. The city underwent the first change in 1594 when a stone wall was built for the fortress, which was only finished in 1713.

In the 17th Century, the city's population was 27,000 people.

Image of Buenos Aires in 1536 (First Foundation).

increase in commercial activity together with smuggling and slaves commerce allowed the city to start expanding rapidly.

INVASIONES INGLESAS.
BRITISH INVASIONS:

In 1800, the British Empire started implementing its colonialist expansion policies. The second step in their plan, after winning the battle in Cabo de la Buena Esperanza, was undertaking the Rio de la Plata area. In 1806, an English commander called Beresford disembarked with his troops in the south of the city. The first British invasion lasted 46 days and Liniers, from Montevideo, planned the recovery of the area. In 1807, another invasion took place and was repelled thanks to a heroic defense carried out by the local population, who later created the first body of Argentinian soldiers, called Patricios.

British troops surrendering to Santiago de Liniers in 1806.

INDEPENDENCIA.
INDEPENDENCE:

In 1810, after the Napoleonic War in Spain, a group of prominent citizens decided to request that the viceroy be dethroned and replaced by an autonomous governing body, the form of which was not still clear.
On July 9, 1816, delegates from both the Capital City and the rest of the country proclaimed absolute independence from the king of Spain.
Once Independence was proclaimed, a fratricidal struggle took place between the city of Buenos Aires and the rest of the provinces in order to determine the system of government for the new nation. In 1850, started growing steadily due to the new political organization in the country. New quarters called Constitución, La Boca and Retiro joined the urban checkerboard. To the west, the city expanded towards a town called Flores and, by 1880, the population had reached 300,000 inhabitants. Health and environmental conditions were not improved as the city grew. Between 1867 and 1871, 20,000 people died of cholera and yellow fever because there was no water system whatsoever and garbage was thrown into the many creeks that ran across the city. When the cholera and yellow fever plagues hit Buenos Aires, the wealthiest families, who lived in the southern areas, were forced to move north.

LA INMIGRACION.
IMMIGRATION:

In 1880, during President Roca's administration, the Federal Capital district of the Argentine Republic was established in the city of Buenos Aires. Torcuato de Alvear, mayor of the city in those times, decided that Buenos Aires should become the Paris of South America. He then had the Old Market (Vieja Recova) demolished, opened Av. De Mayo and developed a new urban area around Av Alvear and Barrio Norte. By 1914, and thanks to emigrants, the city's population had grown eight-fold. The first signals of modern times started to appear in 1920, when the first skyscraper (Barolo building) was built and the first subway lines began working, but it was only in the 1950s that urban development made Buenos Aires one of the biggest cities in the world. During the subsequent decades, the city took its current shape due to the growth of high-rise buildings. In the 1970s, a highway network converging in the city's center was incorporated into Buenos Aires. The error in selection of the converging point caused serious traffic problems, which are accountable for high pollution rates in the downtown area. Nowadays, the city's population is 3 million inhabitants and the number of people living in the suburban area exceeds 9 million.

View of Plaza de Mayo in the middle-18th Century. The main building is the fortress that stood where the Executive Office Building stands today.

View of the port in front of the Customs Building, 1859.

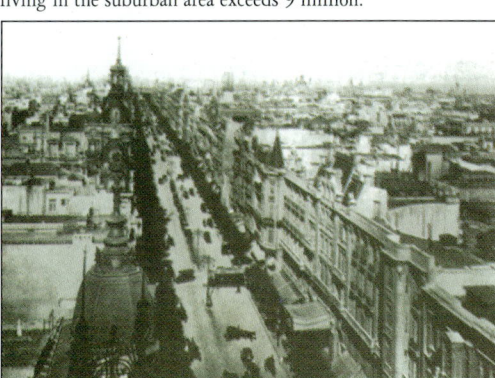

Avenida de Mayo in the early 20th Century.

Recorridos por Buenos Aires.

"The first impression when arriving in Buenos Aires is that of finding the last part of the world which can hold a big city.
In its condition as the last city on Earth, it ends up comprising any other city in the world and reminding us of them.
The second impression is that of the endless. An endlessly big geographical area which is reflected in what is endlessly urban about Buenos Aires..."

Franco Purini

The purpose of this travel guide is to show you the most interesting parts of the city through a visual ride. Although Buenos Aires is an enormous city, the 14 tours we suggest comprise each and every point of interest for those travelers who will spend just a few days in the Capital of Tango.

Tours

1•Plaza de Mayo y alrededores.
2•Catedral al Sur.
3•San Telmo.
4•La Boca.
5•Puerto Madero.
6•Retiro, Centro.
7•Retiro, Alvear.
8•Recoleta.
9•Palermo.
10•Barrio Norte.
11•Av. Corrientes.
12•Plaza Lavalle.
13•Plaza Congreso y las Grandes Cúpulas.
14•Abasto.

Plaza de Mayo and surrounding area

Plaza de Mayo y alrededores

Eva Perón

Mothers of Plaza de Mayo

Plaza de Mayo is the original center of the city's historic area, which was founded by Juan de Garay in 1580.
Ever since 1810 it has been the scene of every major political event in the country. In 1880, Juan Buschiazzo carried out an important remodeling of the square in search of the classical symmetry that can still be recognized there. Some years later, French landscape designer Charles Thays gave the square its current looks. Its surrounding area grew when Av. de Mayo was opened, together with Diagonal Norte and Diagonal Sur streets, and when the City, as we call our downtown area, was developed.
Both in the square and it surrounding area, we can find architectural samples from different periods: the Cabildo, the Pyramid of May and the Cathedral date from the colonial period (18th Century and early 19th Century).
The Executive Office Building (Casa Rosada or Pink House) and the Municipal Building (former Hotel Victoria) date from the late-19th Century /early-20th Century period.
The Ministry of Economy (former Mortgage Bank) and the National Bank buildings belong to the monumental style developed by the government during the 1930s and the 1940s.
Plaza de Mayo was the place where Evita was acclaimed as a political figure and were the Peronist Party was born.
In 1976, during the last coup in Argentina, the square became internationally known due to the presence of the Mothers of Plaza de Mayo, who would walk around the Pyramid every Thursday claiming for their "disappeared" sons and daughters.
In 1983, the square also witnessed the restoration of democracy.
We suggest sitting on one of the benches protected by trees to watch the intense activity in the City and enjoy the views, both of the Obelisk at the end of Diagonal Norte street and of the many belfries and domes along Av. De Mayo.

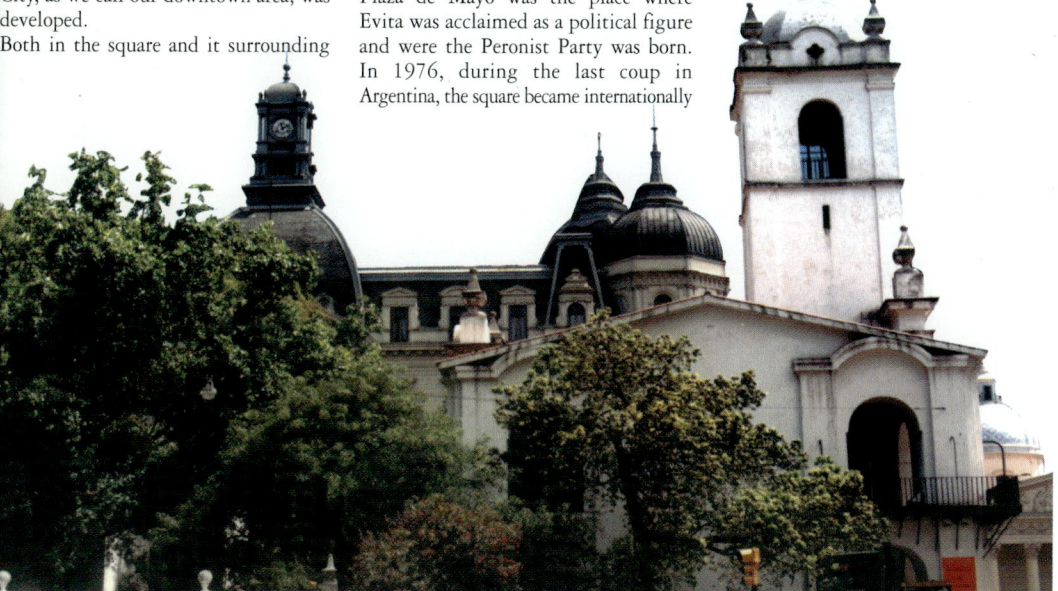

Plaza de Mayo and surrounding area in 3 Dimensions.

Plaza de Mayo y alrededores en 3 Dimensiones.

Manzana de Las Luces or Block of Light (see p. 21).

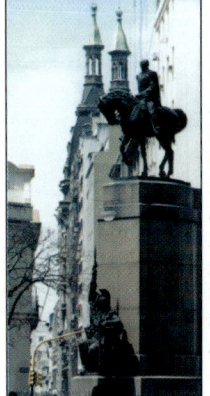

City's Legislature Building (see p. 19).

Equestrian Statue of General Roca: *He directed the conquest of the Patagonic desert, therefore integrating the whole territory of Argentina and exterminating many Native American tribes.*

City's Museum (see p. 24).

Piramide de Mayo. (ver pág. 16).

Ethnography Museum. Juan B. Ambrosetti. Moreno 350.

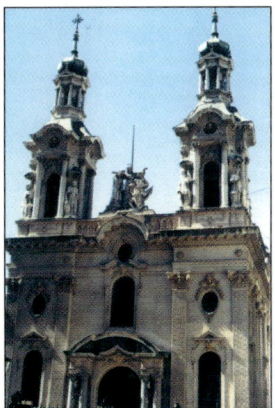

Former Banco Hipotecario or Mortgage Bank.

San Francisco's Convent and Church: *Construction of the Convent started in 1587 and the Church's original building dates from 1754. In the church you may find a beautiful piece of tapestry by visual artist Horacio Butler. The current front of the building was designed in an eclectic style during the late 19th Century. The enormous dome is awesome and it can be seen from the corner of Moreno and Defensa streets. If you take a walk around the block, you will find a group of houses built during the same period. (see p. 16).*

Paseo Colón

Museum of History of the Executive Office Building. *Hipolito Yrigoyen 219. Horario: Lunes a Viernes de 10:00 a 18:00. Free.*

Equestrian Statue of General Belgrano: *It was formally unveiled in 1873 and it was created by French sculptor Albert.*

Plaza Coló

14

Plaza de Mayo and surrounding area

Culture's house ex edificio la prensa.

Cabildo (see p. 16).

City's Executive Office Building.

Corner of Diagonal Norte and Florida streets: *You may find huge domes and an interesting neocolonial building owned by the Bank of Boston with a shocking entrance door and hall in Plateresque style. If you walk down Florida street, you will get to San Martin Square and Retiro.*

Rivadavia

Diagonal Roque Saenz Peña

Florida St.

San Martín

Catedral Metropolitana: *(See p.17).*

Reconquista

National Bank of Argentina.

Leandro N. Alem

Monument to Cristobal Colón.

Executive Office Building (Casa Rosada or Pink House): *It is built on the site chosen by Garay for the city's fortress in 1580. The building has undergone many changes. In 1882, two twin buildings were the seat of the Executive Office and they were later joined by means of an archway which is now the main entrance, looking on Plaza de Mayo. In 1873, President Sarmiento had it painted pink and it remained so until now.*

15

Plaza de Mayo and surrounding area

El Cabildo

The Cabildo

It was originally the seat of the city's government and its construction finished in 1764. At the back of the Cabildo there is a big patio where the jail for male prisoners used to be.

When Av. De Mayo was opened, in 1889, a third of the original building was demolished and the same thing happened again when Diagonal Sur street was created. The cabildo was of great importance during the events that led to the proclamation of independence from Spanish rule in 1810. Its current appearance should be thanked to a detailed restoration work undertaken in 1939. In the patio behind the building, you will find a walkway that joins Hipólito Yrigoyen street with Av de Mayo. This is the ideal place to take a break and breathe the air of colonial Buenos Aires.

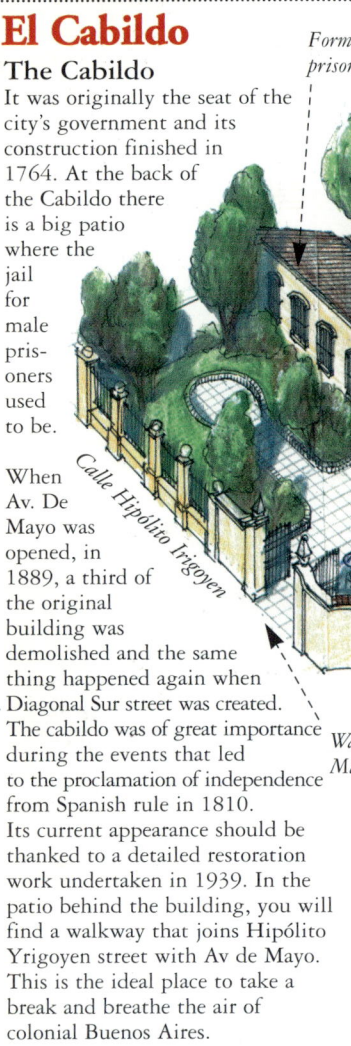

Former jail for male prisoners.
Colonial patio.
Av. de Mayo
Calle Hipólito Yrigoyen
Walkway to Av de Mayo.
Museum's ticket office.
Entrance to Museum.

Inside the Cabildo there is a small crafts fair and an inexpensive fast-food restaurant.

Visiting Times: *Tuesday through Friday: 12:30 to 7 PM. Sundays: 3 PM to 7 PM. Guided tours on Sundays at 4 PM.*

Cabildo: *From Plaza de Mayo you may see the unfinished appearance of the building.*

Pyramid of May: *It was erected in 1811 to commemorate the events of May 1810. The original structure is still inside the current pyramid. It was created by Francisco Cañete.*

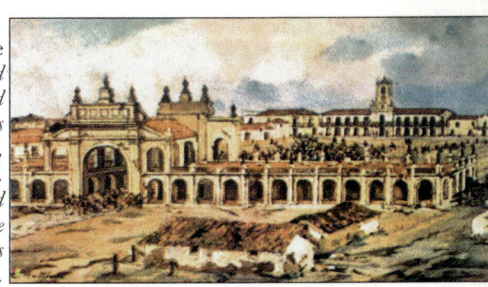

View of Plaza de Mayo: *(around 1810) The old market, which was demolished in 1882, is on the foreground. On the background you may see the Cabildo with its original archways.*

16

Plaza de Mayo and surrounding area

La Catedral

The Cathedral

The original building dates from 1745 and the facade was modified in 1821 when a neoclassical gate was introduced according to the French trends of the time.
It was designated as Cathedral in 1836, once Joseph Dubourdieu had finished the magnificent new facade, which represents Jacob with his son, Joseph. (You may see it from the square across the street).
If you enter the building and walk along the nave to your right, when you get to the fourth column you will find a chapel containing the mausoleum of General San Martín. Soldiers of the Granaderos corps, a branch of the army created by General San Martín himself, permanently guard the site. Next to the first column on the right nave you may see a Russian icon, Our Lady of Vladimir, and also an image of Our Lady of the Forsaken, which was created in Sevilla during the 18th Century. Both the alta piece on the main altar and the paintings in it date from the late 18th Century period.

Guided tours: *Monday through Friday at 1 PM. Saturdays at 11:30 AM. Sundays at 10 A.M. Meeting point: entrance to the nave on your right.*

Main altarpiece, 18th Century.

Altarpiece of the Main Altar: *Icon of the Immaculate Virgin. 18th Century.*

Mausoleum of General San Martín.

Meeting point for guided tours.

These twelve columns represent the twelve Apostles.

General San Martín: *He is the most important Argentinian hero. Liberator of the American continent, he is called "Father of the Nation".*

Icon of Our Lady of the Forsaken, late 18th Century.

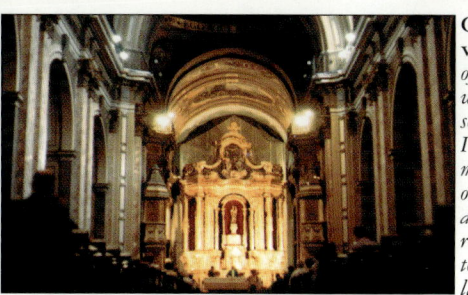

Cathedral (inside view): *The inside of the Cathedral was designed in a sober baroque style. In the picture you may see the rich ornaments in the altar, which was recently restored together with all the lateral chapels.*

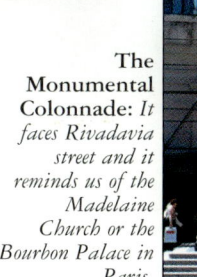

The Monumental Colonnade: *It faces Rivadavia street and it reminds us of the Madelaine Church or the Bourbon Palace in Paris.*

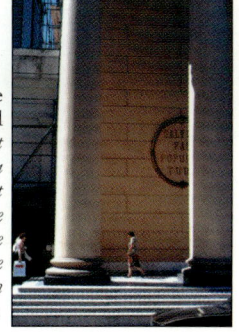

17

Plaza de Mayo and surrounding area

Avenida de Mayo entre Perú y Plaza de Mayo.

Av de Mayo between Perú street and Plaza de Mayo.
Former building of "La Prensa" (newspaper) and current House of Culture.
In 1910, after a visit to Buenos Aires, George Clemenceau said: "Undoubtedly, the most sumptuous building is that of the opulent La Prensa, which is known to be the main newspaper in South America".
In a prominently French style, you may see superb pieces of blacksmithing on gates and lamps. The inside of the entrance hall has recently been restored and it has recovered its famous original decoration, which is well worth a visit, as well as the Golden Hall on the first floor, where concerts and other cultural events are usually held.

Florida street.
London cafeteria.
La Prensa building.
Executive Office Building for the City of Buenos Aires.
Av. de Mayo
Pasaje Roverano, connection with Perú subway station.
Perú Station, Subway Line A.
Plaza de Mayo

La Prensa building entrance gate.

Facade of La Prensa building.

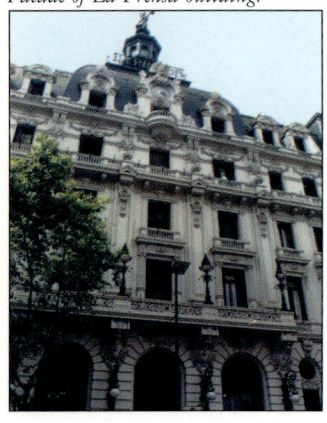

Perú subway station and Passage Roverano
On the same side of the street as the building of La Prensa you will find a subway station that belonged to the first subway line in Latin America. This station has been restored to its original condition by the City's Museum. A visit to Perú station will carry you to the Buenos Aires of the 1910s.
If you walk across Av de Mayo from La Prensa building, you will see an interesting passage called Pasaje Roverano, which is connected with the subway station. You may find the connection by entering the passage's ground floor (see picture).
Cortázar and The Winners
On the corner of Perú street and

View of Av de Mayo.

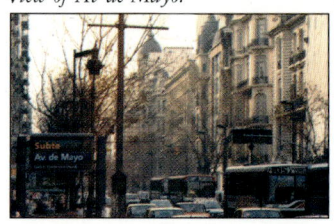

Julio Cortázar, Argentinian writer.

Av de Mayo there stands a Liberty-style building that conveys a London-like atmosphere. The name of the cafeteria in the building is precisely London and it is an old and traditional shop, which has unfortunately been modernized.
Part of the action in Julio Cortázar's novel "The Winners" develops in this cafeteria.
Across Perú street, you may see a real display of luxurious buildings in a wide variety of Italian, French and Victorian styles. We suggest that you take a walk along Pasaje Urquiza Anchorena (on the odd-numbered sidewalk at 600). This passage joins Av de Mayo and Rivadavia street.

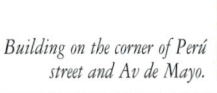
Building on the corner of Perú street and Av de Mayo.

Plaza de Mayo and surrounding area

Legislatura de la Ciudad de Buenos Aires.

Legislature Building of the City of Buenos Aires

This building was erected in 1930 by Architect Héctor Ayerza. It covers a big plot between Diagonal Sur street and Perú street and it is a sample of the eclectic trends in architecture during the first decades of this century. Its imposing neoclassical facade stretches along Diagonal Sur street and Perú street.

It has a very big and cozy library and there are also some halls designed for exhibitions on the ground floor. Halls San Martín and El Dorado, which have been recently restored, deserve a visit.

The tower is almost 90 meters high and on top of it there is a unique carillon for a clock that is still at work.

90-meter tower with carillon.

Perú

Representatives Chamber.

Entrance to library.

Diagonal Julio A. Roca

Entrance to exhibition halls.

Main entrance to halls.

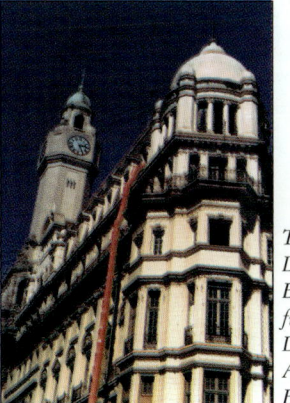

Tower of the Legislature Building as seen from the corner of Diagonal Julio A Roca and Bolívar streets.

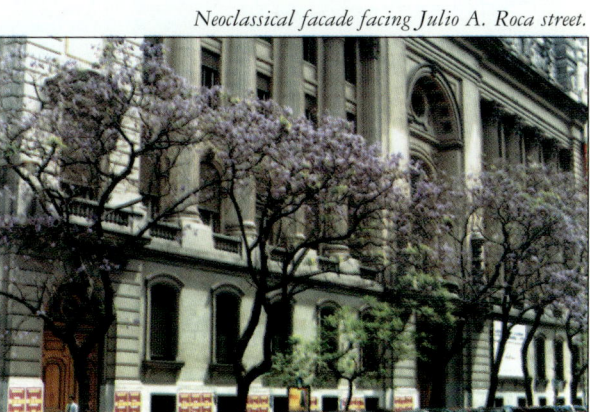

Neoclassical facade facing Julio A. Roca street.

Plaza de Mayo and surrounding area

Facade of San Ignacio's Church: *It was built in 1675. Inside the church you may find many altarpieces and pieces of imagery that date from the colonial period. Pay special attention to the rose stained-glass window at the back of the church.*

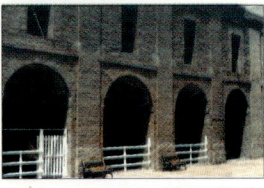

Archways, patio and vault of Procuraduría de las Misiones.

View of the Manzana de las Luces or Block of Light. In the late 18th Century.

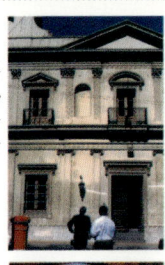

Neoclassical facade, 19th Century. Entrance to the cloisters of the Procuratie of the Missions (Procuraduría de las Misiones).

Inside view of San Ignacio's Church.

SAN FRANCISCO CHURCH AND MONASTERY. SAN ROQUE PARISH.

On Alsina and Defensa Streets. It was built in 1730 by Jesuit architect Bianchi. Its final reconstruction was made by Arq. Sackmann in a German Barroc style. Some statues of San Francisco de Asís, Giotto, Dante Alighieri and Cristóbal Colón are placed on its facade. In the inner part, people can see a XX century tapestry made by argentine artist Horacio Buttler, containing a Virgin image, Franciscans tree, and San Francisco surrounded by animals and mendicants. San Roque Parish is one of the oldest churches in the city and it has a very important and valuable library.

SAN FRANCISCO SMALL SQUARE:

It was built to give shelter to the great quantity of people who remained after religious ceremonies at San Francisco Church. The four statues which were located surrounding May Pyramid, have been replaced here at 1972 and they represent the Geography, Sailing, Astronomy and Industry.

Tapíz.(8x12 meters), work of the painter Horacio Butler.

20

Plaza de Mayo and surrounding area

Manzana de la Luces.
Block of Light.

The block is limited by the following streets: Perú, Alsina, Bolívar and Moreno. In 1616, this land was given to the Jesuits, who built San Ignacio's School and Church there. The church is currently at the corner of Bolívar and Alsina streets. The School of the Society of Jesus was demolished and the National School of Buenos Aires was derected on the site, where it still stands today as the most traditional and prestigious school in the city.

The cloisters of the Procuraduría de las Misiones, which date from the late-17th Century period (the oldest in the city), stand on Perú street as well as the houses in numbers 222, 274 and 294. The Jesuits were evicted in 1767 and the land was used for different purposes, such as location for the National School and University. These were the places were most of the intellectuals and literati that took part in the events leading to Argentinian Independence were educated. That is the reason why, in 1821, the area was called Manzana de las Luces (Block of Light) as a way to honor the men and women of letters who were educated there.

We suggest that you start your visit at San Ignacio's Church, which was put up on the corner of Bolívar and Alsina streets in 1675. After that, you may visit the National School of Buenos Aires. It was built in 1911 and its monumental size is typically inspired by classical architecture. When you turn right at the corner of Bolívar and Moreno streets, you will find a colonial facade that belongs to the above-mentioned houses. When you get to Perú street, you may wish to turn right and enter number 277, which has recently been restored and holds the former Representatives Chamber.

If you keep on walking along Perú street, you will find, in number 222, the oldest building in the block, which used to belong to the Procuraduría de las Misiones. As you approach the corner of Perú street and Diagonal Sur, you may find the entrance to a handicrafts market.

Another interesting spot you might wish to visit in the Block of Light is that of the tunnels which run under it.

Former Representatives Chamber.
Perú St.
Courtyard of the Procuraduría.
Moreno St.
Diagonal South.
National School of Buenos Aires.
Handicrafts market.
Bolívar St.
Alsina St.
San Ignacio Church.

Map of the tunnels in the 18th Century, 6 meters underground.

They were built around 6 meters deep by the Jesuits in the 18th Century and they used to connect Jesuit temples with strategic places in the city.

Guided Tours: *Fridays at 3 PM (free). Saturdays at 3 PM and 4:30 PM. Sundays at 3 PM, 4 PM and 5 PM. Meeting point: Perú 272.*

21

Plaza de Mayo and surrounding area

Av. de Mayo y sus puntos de interés.
Av de Mayo and its interesting spots.

Plaza de Mayo and surrounding area

El café Tortoni. Tortoni coffee.

Av. de Mayo

Bust of Juan de Dios Filiberto by Luis Perlotti.

National Academy of Tango.

Cultural Vault, basement.

Bust of Benito Quinquela Martín.

Bust of Borges.

Bust of Julián Centella by Antonio Pujía.

Poets' Corner.

Tourist Information Office.

Shows area.

Rivadavia Street

Alfonsina STORNI

Federico Garcia LORCA

Jorge Luis BORGES

Our traditional Tortoni Café is located at the odd side of the street on Av de Mayo between Tacuarí and Piedras streets. It was one of the first cafés in the city and it used to be the meeting point for intellectuals and politicians. Nowadays, it serves as a real cultural center where jazz and tango events are usually held.

If you take a leisurely walk inside the café and pay attention to the walls, you may find several commemorative objects for famous personalities of the arts, which have been placed in the spots where those people used to sit. Thus, you will see them over the tables at which Jorge Luis Borges, painter Quinquela Martín, poet and journalist Roberto Arlt, Federico García Lorca, poet Alfonsina Storni and others used to sit.

In the basement of an adjoining building we find what we call La Bodega or The Vault, a kind of café where shows are staged and where you will have the opportunity to listen to some excellent tango music. The National Academy of Tango, the muse of which is poet Horacio Ferrer, is on the ground floor of the same building. You may enter through the door next to Tortoni Café. At the back of the café, there is a small library called El Rincón de los Poetas, or Poets' Corner, where the city government has installed a tourist information office.

The café has two entrance doors: one of the faces Av de Mayo and the other one, Rivadavia street. If you go out through the second door, you will find Roberto Arlt Square across the street. This is another oasis where you will be able to forget the buzzing of the city for a moment. Behind the palos borrachos and other species of indigenous vegetation, you will have the opportunity to admire a huge mural in relief by visual artist Alberto Cedrón. The apse you will see from the square belongs to San Miguel Arcángel Church.

23

City's Museum

El Museo de la Ciudad.

On the corner of Defensa and Alsina streets (Alsina 412) there stands the City's Museum. The building is a good sample of how a bourgeois house looked like by the end of the 19th Century. The Museum serves an important purpose, since it keeps the urban memories of the city alive through several restoration and preservation activities (see Perú subway station). On the first floor, the Museum usually exhibits interesting pieces of its collection depicting uses and customs of the city's population. On the ground floor, a drugstore called La Estrella (The Star) has been preserved in its original condition, as it looked when it was the Old Pharmacy of the area. On the same sidewalk of Alsina street, next door to the Museum, you will find Puerto Rico cafeteria, a perfect spot to take a break.

Articles rescued from demolition sites by the Museum.

Household appliances from the Museum's collection. Inside view of the Museum.

City's Museum on the corner of Alsina and Defensa streets.

Opening time: Monday through Friday: 11 AM to 7 PM. Sundays: 3 PM to 7 PM. Special thanks to Eduardo Vazquez.

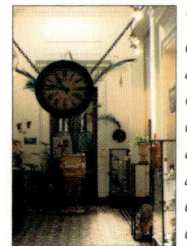

The Museum holds exhibitions of everyday articles in their original condition and even objects taken from demolition sites acquire a high value when they enter the Museum's collection.

ETNOGRAPHIC MUSEUM JUAN B. AMBROSETTI.

On 350 Moreno St. It was created by Philosophy and Letters School in 1904. It has a valuable archeological collection from Argentine Patagonia and NorthWest, and from Africa and Oceanía. The building was built at 1876 by Arq. Pedro Benoit to Law School of Buenos Aires University. The museum is located here from 1928.

Library.
Offices and shops.
Exposition rooms.

24

South of the Cathedral

Catedral al Sur.

In the area bound by Plaza de Mayo and San Telmo quarter there are many places of interest as well as some streets and passages that stand out due to their shape.
The block called Santo Domingo was the area where a crucial battle took place during the British Invasion (see p. 26).
If you walk along Balcarce street and cross Belgrano Avenue until you arrive at Independencia street, you will pass by some of the best places where you can enjoy tango shows, dance and have dinner. They all open in the evening. We suggest that you have a drink and relax in some of the bars at the corner of Chile and Balcarce streets, it will allow you to penetrate the quiet atmosphere of the city's southern neighborhoods.

Catedral al Sur en 3 Dimensiones.

Martín Fierro: José Hernández (1834-1886), an Argentinian poet and journalist born in Buenos Aires, is the author of Martín Fierro, a folk epic poem that is considered a national classic in Argentina.

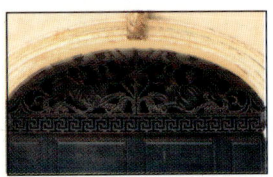

Detail of the entrance gate to José Hernandez's house.

Former National Library and current National Hall of Music: In this enormous neoclassical building, Borges worked as the director of the National Library for many years. It stands on Mexico street, between Bolívar and Perú streets.

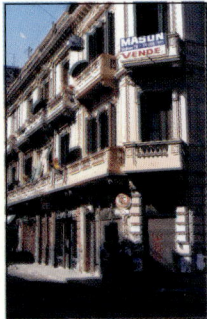

Typical house with balconies on the corner of Defensa and San Lorenzo streets. This area is crowded with artists' studios, thus making up the Argentinian Montmartre.

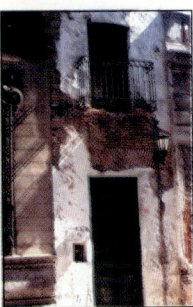

When you walk along San Lorenzo passage, you will find a narrow house that is called the "tiny house". It is only 2.30 meters wide.

The corner of Chile and Balcarce streets is the perfect spot to take a break. On the background, you may see the building of Antorchas, a foundation that promotes the arts.

San Lorenzo's Passage: Principled house of the 19th century.

Catedral al Sur

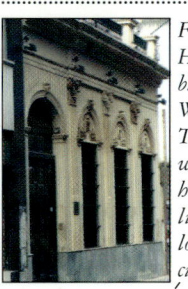

Former house of José Hernández and current building of the Argentine Writer's Association. Typical one-story house with a row of patios. It houses an important library and serves as location for several cultural activities.

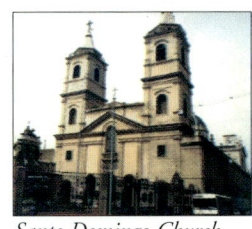

Santo Domingo Church. (See p. 28)

Sample of fantastic architecture with esoteric symbols, near the corner of Bolívar and Chile streets.

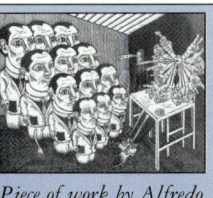

Piece of work by Alfredo Benavídez Bedoya, Argentinian engraver.

Museum of Engraving: a large old house at Defensa 372 serves as seat for the Museum of Engraving. It has collections of Argentinian engravers from the 19th and 20th Century on display. The institution carries out an intense activity and it regularly organizes exhibitions.

Opening time:
Monday through Saturday: 2 PM to 6 PM. Sundays: 12 to 6 PM. Guided tours: Sundays at 3 PM.

We suggest that you walk by number 350 Defensa street, next to the Museum of Engraving. There stands the house of Bernardino Rivadavia, the first president of Argentina, in its original condition (18th Century).

General Belgrano, designer of the Argentinian flag. His tomb is in the atrium of Santo Domingo Church.

27

Balcarce Street: Tango

Calle Balcarce: Tanguerías.

Michelangelo, *Restaurant, Tango.*

Moliere, *Cofee, Restaurant, Bar, Tango.*

Taconeando, *Tango.*

La Trastienda, *show.*

La ventana, *Restaurant, Tango, Show.*

Casa Blanca, *Dinner, Tango, Show.*

OUR LADY OF ROSARIO BASILIC. SANTO DOMINGO CONVENT.

Belgrano Av. and Defensac st. Its construction began in 1751 under the direction of Architect Antonio Masella. One of the towers was inaugurated at the end of XVIII century and the other one at the middle of last century. It keeps English flags, taken during English Invasions when they occupied the church and the flags from the royalists that Belgrano donated to the Virgin. Mausoleum of Gral Belgrano is located from the beginning of this century, in the atrium of the church. This is a work of Italian sculptor Ettore Ximenes.
On the left tower, people can see replicas of the shots in 1807, because it has been reconstructed.

Cannon bullets, fingerprints of the English Invasions.

Monumental staircase called De Los Ingleses.

University of the North, Santo Tomás de Aquino

Organ.

Mausoleum of Manuel Belgrano designer of the Argentine flag.

Dressing-room of the Virgin. Chapel where are kept trophies of the reconquest of the city of Buenos Aires in 1807.

San Telmo Quarter.

San Telmo

Our tour along the southern area of Buenos Aires continues along Defensa street until we get to Independencia Avenue, where we enter the San Telmo quarter. This quarter was born in 1735 as a hamlet in the outskirts of the city. Where Dorrego Square stands today, there used to be a residence for the Bethlehemite monks, south of the Lezama ranch (today, Museum of History and park).

The quarter's population was made up of aristocratic families until 1870, when they moved to the northern area of the city escaping the plagues partly caused by the poor health conditions in Buenos Aires. San Telmo then became a residential neighborhood and, in time, the large houses started to serve as tenement houses or conventillos where immigrants used to rent rooms, which led to growing deterioration of the buildings during the first half of the 20th Century.

It was only in the 1970s that some rules were established in order to preserve the quarter's buildings, thus keeping valuable pieces of architecture from damage. Nowadays, the area is plenty of antique shops, especially along Defensa street, between Independencia and San Juan avenues. This is the perfect place for a walk on Sundays, since there is an antiques fair in Dorrego Square (on the corner of Defensa and Carlos Calvo streets) every Sunday morning, opening at 10 AM. (See p. 33).

29

San Telmo en 3 Dimensiones.

Lezama Park.

It is the highest area along the riverbanks. During the 17th Century, it was used as an area for warehouses and slave cabins. It later became the ranch of the Lezama family and, in 1884, the whole plot was purchased by the city's government and used to build a park we can visit nowadays. It was restored recently and it houses a sculpture garden and a watchtower.

British Bar (Bar Británico): *It is a mythical spot of Buenos Aires, crowded by artists and bohemians, the perfect place for the sleepless, since it is always open. Right across the street you will find Hipopótamus Bar, which is quite similar to the British Bar.*

Russian Orthodox Church: *In front of the park you may see the Russian Orthodox Church, an exotic building with five onion-shaped domes erected in the early-20th Century period.*

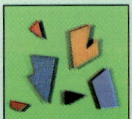

Work by Raúl Lozza, Museum's collection.

Museum of Modern Art: *It houses important painting and sculpture collections of contemporary art, both from Argentina and from abroad. Exhibitions are regularly organized in the Museum. It had many famous directors, it was founded by Rafael Squirru and it gained dynamism and prestige during Raúl Santana's administration, a period during which great exhibitions were held, such as that of the Cobra group. The building used to be a tobacco storehouse and it was restored to serve as a museum.*

Opening time: *Monday through Friday from 10 AM to 8 PM. Saturdays, Sundays and Public Holidays from 11 AM to 8 PM.*
Guided tours: *for the public in general, Tuesday through Sunday at 5 PM; for institutions: request in advance by phone. Ticket price: $ 1. Wednesdays free in both wings.*

San Telmo

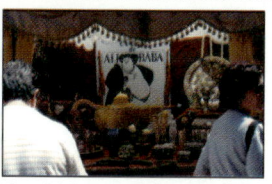

San Telmo's Fair: *It is held every Sunday from 10 Am to 6 PM in Dorrego Square and adjoining streets. You may go and purchase antiques or small works of art, or you may just mingle with people and be entertained by street performers and tango dancers.*

Forner-Bigatti Foundation: *Facing Dorrego Square there is a house that dates from the 1930s, an example of rationalist architecture. It was the place of abode of Raquel Forner and Alfredo Bigatti, two well-known visual artists from Argentina.*

San Pedro Telmo's Church: *(See P. 33)*

Bar Dorrego: *Humberto Primo and Defensa st.. It is the most traditional and well-known bar in the area. Inside of the bar you may breathe the atmosphere of a typical tavern of the 1920s.*

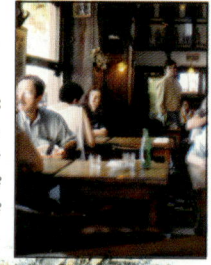

Song for Labor, *sculpture by Rogelio Yrurtia. The author was one of Rodin's disciples and he is known as one of the most important Latin American sculptors. (The work may be seen in the piazza located at the corner of Paseo Colón and Independencia Avenue).*

Former Eva Perón Foundation and current College of Engineering: *This building was designed during a military government in the 1930s and it is a typical example of German neoclassical architecture. It was built in the 1940s and it served as the seat of Eva Perón Foundation, the purpose of which was to aid the poor.*

31

San Telmo

Pasaje de los Ezeiza

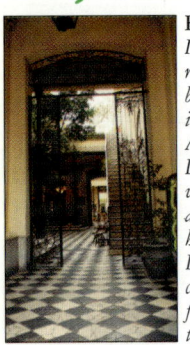

House of the Ezeiza family.
*It was built around 1880 and it has a row of several patios. This kind of buildings were called "sausage houses" in Buenos Aires and they were an Argentinian version of the old Roman Domus as adapted to plots of land that were just 11 meters wide. It also served as a typical tenement house that could hold a maximum of 32 families.
It was restored in 1982 and it became a commercial passage. Today, you may find antique shops and souvenir stores that sell posters and cards.*

courtyard of the cistern

courtyard of the Tree

María de San Telmo: *store that sells articles for tourists, such as travel guides, posters, cards and souvenirs.*

courtyard of the Time

San Pedro Telmo's Church.

CHURCH OF OUR LADY OF BELÉN & SAN PEDRO GONZALEZ TELMO:
On Humberto I° St. 340.
The construction of the church began in 1734 on the project plan by the jesuit architect brother Andrés Blanqui and the support of the brothers Juan Bautista Prímoli and José Schmidt and who finished the construction was the Italian master Antonio Masella; the last restauration was made by Pelayo Sáinz in 1918. The front was made in eclectic style, with some architectonic elements of Neo Colonial and Barroc styles and in the upper part St. Peter Gonzalez Telmo´s image has been located. It has been recognized as National Historical Monument.

Dome with coating of Stone.

Dome of plant of eight side.

ARGENTINE PENITENTIARY MUSEUM "ANTONIO BALLVÉ":
378, Humberto I° St.
The museum is an 1760 building and the plans were made by the architect Antonio Masella. At the first time, it had been the Spiritual Retreat House for men. In 1767, when Jesuit Order was sent off, City Hall established here Women Jail under the supervision of Penitentiary Service until 1978 when the jail was moved to the neighbourhood of Ezeiza. The Our Lady of Carmen Chapel, an 1734 construction, is located inside this museum.

Porch and facade neoclasic, ended in 1942.

Access to the penitentiary museum.

Jesuit Oratory.

Courtyard of the 18th century.

Dorrego Square in 3 Dimensions

Plaza Dorrego en 3 Dimensiones.

DORREGO SQUARE:
Between Humberto I, Defensa, Anselmo Aieta and Bethlem Streets. It was declared of National Historical Interest because this is where the people met to reconfirm their Declaration of Independence from Spain. Dorrego is the oldest square in the city after Plaza de Mayo Sq. On Sundays from 10.00 to 17.00 hs. an Antique Market functions here organized by City Museum, while the Square seems to go back into the past and dancers move to the sound of Tangos and Milongas.

Almacén de Tangos Generales: store that sells posters and souvenirs.

Antique shop specialized in phonographs and old record players on the corner of Bethlen and Defensa streets.

Dorrego Bar, on the corner of Defensa and Carlos Calvo streets.

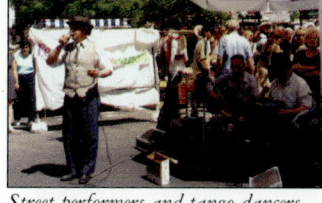

Housing building accomplished by the architects Poblet and Ortuzar of academic style, about 1920s.

Foundation Forner Bigati. Raquel Forner and Alfredo Bigati were two greit Argentine artists. This house was their shop.

Street performers and tango dancers on the corner of Defensa and Carlos Calvo streets.

LEZAMA PARK:

- Amphitheatre.
- Looking.
- Sculptures courtyard.
- Russian Orthodox Church.
- Britanic Bar.
- Monument Source to Sir Pedro de Mendoza.
- National Historical Museum.
- Monument to the International fraternity.

National Museum of History

El Museo Histórico Nacional

The national Museum of History building used to be the house of the Lezama family. Its appearance is similar to that of an Italian palazzo, with a square-shaped tower that dominated the southern area of the city for many years.
Its 32 rooms made up one of the most important residences during the first half of the 19th Century. In 1897, the building was assigned to the National Museum of History, founded by Adolfo Carranza. The Museum's collection shows us a panoramic view of the history of Argentina since the 16th Century until the end of the 19th Century.
A special room devoted to General San Martín houses a reproduction of his room in Grand Bourg, France.

Relics from the Jesuits' missions and trophies from the battle of Suipacha are also on display. The Museum also has an important collection of drawings and paintings by travelling artists of the 19th Century, such as French painter Palliere, Italian artist Pellegrini and French engraver Gericault. Undoubtedly, the main work of art in this collection is a series of paintings on the War of Paraguay by Cándido López.

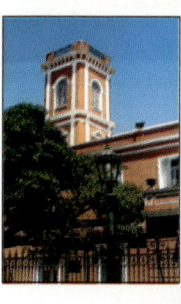
Square-shaped tower that dominates the museum's building.

Opening times:
Tuesday through Friday, from 2 PM to 6 PM. Saturdays and Sundays from 3 PM to 7 PM. Admission: free.

Five domes carried in metal.

Crossings watching to the East hold with chains.

Pulpits.

Icon of the Santísima Trinidad.

Choir

Access staircase to the Shrine that this in the first floor.

Altar watching to the East.

RUSSIAN ORTHODOX CHURCH OF THE HOLY TRINITY:

315 Brasil St. between Defensa and Paseo Colón Streets.
This church was opened in 1904; the original project was made by the architect of Russian Holy Synod, Mihail Preobrazensky, and was adapted by the architect Alejandro Christophersen. The temple was built in Muscovite style of XVII century.

San Telmo

Detail of a painting by José Bouche that depicts a Spaniard fraternizing with a Native American woman.

Oil painting by F. Augero, 1865. Battle between Native Americans and national guard forces.

Engraving, 1794. It depicts and Argentinian cowboy or "gaucho" catching a cow with his rope.

18th-Century board engraved in the Jesuits' missions.

Also in the Museum's garden, a collection of cannons and bells from different periods.

"Maipú Battle", lithography by Gericault, 1819.

Opening of the first railway system (August 30, 1857).

Entrance gate with archways in typical Italian style.

"View of Curuzú", oil painting by Cándido López.

"Review by Río Negro", oil painting by Juan Manuel Blanes.

35

La Boca Quarter

La Boca

The origin of this quarter is undoubtedly connected with the Rivulet or Riachuelo, on the banks of which it started to develop.

The activity brought about by the river, the increase in trade, the presence of shipyards and other factors attracted people who settled down in this area of the city. It was not long before emigrants started to move into the quarter. Most of them came from Genoa, in Italy, and therefore, by 1870, la Boca had already acquired its own shape. It still remains as the only part of the city that has a close relationship with the river.

The heart of the quarter is Caminito street, a narrow pedestrian passage almost 100 meters long which was built on an old stretch for rails and took its name from a famous tango song by Juan de Dios Filiberto. The typical houses in this area are made up of formed sheet metal and most of them have become either tenement houses or painters' studios. Their characteristic colorful walls arise from an project designed by painter Benito Quinquela Martín, who thought that painting the walls in different colors would give Caminito a definite character. If you walk along the rivulet's bank, you will come across Nicolás Avellaneda bridge, which offers a full panoramic view of the area and the river. Next to this bridge stands the old transporter bridge, which was built in 1908 and is currently abandoned.

La Boca Quarter

Calle Caminito • Caminito Street

Bas-relief on popular topics in Caminito Street.

PROA Foundation.

Caminito Street.

In Caminito street there is an outdoors museum with sculptures, engravings and mural paintings on popular issues. Besides, visual artists offer their small pieces of art for sale at low prices and most of their work focuses on the neighborhood and on tango culture.. In the surrounding area there are lots of souvenir shops.

OPENING TIME
*Monday to Sundays: of 9 to 19 hs.
Admission Free.*

De la Ribera Theater

Handicraft fair.

Riachuelo.

Old Transporter Bridge.

Nicolas Avellaneda Bridge.

Original houses on the corner of Magallanes and Garibaldi streets.

38

La Boca quarter.

Estadio del Cub Atletico Boca Juniors.

BRANDSEN

Del Valle Iberlucea

Vuelta de Rocha.

Puerto de Palos.

La Perla Bar: traditional business in the city, on the corner of Pedro de Mendoza and del Valle Ibarlucea streets.

Voluntary Firemans quarter

Martin Rodriguez.

Av. Almirante Brown

San Juan Evangelista Church

In the entrance to Caminito street, you will find street performers and many couples of tango dancers.

Old barges and tugboats remain stranded in Vuelta de Rocha, which used to be a dynamic commercial port in front of Caminito.

Benito Quinquela Martín School and Museum, located at Pedro de Mendoza 1835.

La Boca Quarter

Estadio del Club Boca Juniors

Boca Juniors Soccer Stadium
La Boca quarter is closely related to the history of Boca Juniors Soccer Club, the most popular one in the city. Due to its vertical structure that seems to go beyond the sidewalk's limits, the stadium is called La Bombonera, that is, The Chocolate Box. It can hold barely more than 50,000 spectators.

Near the stadium, on the corner of Brandsen and Del Valle Iberlucea streets, there are two well-known, excellent restaurants: la Cancha and El Carlitos. Further away from the stadium, in number 64 of Cafarena street, you will find another restaurant called El Obrero.

The area that stretches along Necochea street between Brandsen and Olavarría streets is crowded with canteens that buzz with activity in the evening.

Fundación Proa. Proa Foundation.

It organizes many cultural activities. Its rooms have served as exhibition halls for paintings of major local and international artists, such as German painter and photographer Anselm Kiefer, and Mexican painter Julio Galán.

"While I Wake Up", oil painting by Julio Galán.

La Boca Quarter.

Escuela Museo Quinquela Martín

Quinquela Martín School and Museum
On the higher floors of Quinquela Martín Elementary School you will find the Museum of Painting and Sculpture.
Its founder, Benito Quinquela Martín, intended to show in its great collection not only the work of painters from La Boca but also that of many Argentinian artists from the first half of this Century. Among them, it is worth mentioning Quinquela Martín himself, Fortunato Lacámera, Policastro, Spilimbergo, Victorica, Sívori, Gramajo Guitiérrez and Rodolfo Cascales.
On the third floor of the building, which has a superb watchtower that overlooks Vuelta de Rocha, we will find the apartment where Quinquela Martín worked and lived until the end of his life, in 1972. Upon his death, he left the whole building, including De La Ribera Theater next door, to the city's government.

"Barges", oil painting by Quinquela Martín.

"From my studio", oil painting by Fortunato Lacámera.

Quinquela. *Filiberto.* *Lacamera.*

Shop of the painter Quinquela Martin in the 1th finish floor, looking.

Terrace, sculptures exposition.

Rooms of permanent exposition.

room of the Mascarones.

Opening time: Tuesday through Friday from 8 AM to 5:30 PM. Saturdays and Sundays from 8 AM to 12 and from 1 PM to 5:30 PM. Admission: free. Address. Pedro de Mendoza 1835.

In the Hall of the theatre there are two important oils of Quinquela.

Ribera Theatre.

"The Utopia of my Neighborhood", sculpture by Ricardo Longhini.

Nowadays, many painters and sculptors live and work in La Boca, which allows the quarter to preserve its tradition as a neighborhood of artists and bohemians. These are just some samples of those artists' work.

"The Model", oil painting by Leopoldo Presas.

"Mirador", acrylic painting by Rómulo Macció.

41

Puerto Madero

In 1880, the city's government began to build a new port, which was later given the name Port Madero in honor of Engineer Eduardo Madero, its designer.

The project turned out to be quite similar to that of the docklands in London, with four closed and connected docks which are placed parallel to the river. In 1910, the port was already too small for the needs of a city that had increasingly gained a greater commercial activity. It was then that the so-called New Port (Puerto Nuevo) was built north of Puerto Madero. As years went by, Puerto Madero was abandoned but, in the early 1990s, a redevelopment project was carried out and the whole port became a promenade, with apartments, offices and recreation areas.

In the old redeveloped warehouses you will find a great number of restaurants (quite expensive), movie theaters, drugstores and even a University campus.

We suggest that you take a walk along the docklands. The area is very attractive, both during the day and in the evening.

If you walk along Brasil street towards the river, you will pass by Ernesto de la Cárcova Art School, where you may visit the Museum of Compared Sculpture (see p. 45) and, if you turn left when you get to Costanera Avenue, you will find Las Nereidas Fountain and the Biological Reserve (see p. 45).

Puerto Madero, Dock I and II

Puerto Madero Dique I y II

Museo de Calcos y Esculturas comparadas.

Museum of Tracing and Compared Sculpture: It is inside Ernesto de la Cárcova Art School. In the museum's rooms you will find direct reproductions of the main sculptures in the history of art. They were brought to Argentina in the beginning of this Century and, among them, we can mention some of Michelangelo's pieces (see David in the picture). When you visit the museum, you will also find perfect tracings of Egyptian relieves. Finally, we suggest that you take a walk on the cozy gardens at the back of the school, which are plenty of sculptures and mural paintings.

Catholic University of Argentina.
Movie Theatre
Dique I
Av. Brasil

Biological Reserve: One of the entrance areas is next to the pier, in front of Las Nereidas Fountain. When the debris collected in demolitions was thrown to the river for leveling purposes, an ecosystem similar to the one that existed when the city was founded started to develop. In the Reserve, you will find a rich variety of fish species and a wide range of wild ducks, otters and other small animals. It gives you an opportunity to know the Pampas just a few blocks from the city's downtown area.

Puerto Madero

The newly restored warehouses in Puerto Madero have preserved their original appearance for the most part. They are solid buildings made up of clay bricks in English style and they house pricey lofts that may be used as either offices or apartments. When you walk along the riverbank, you might wish to visit the Uruguay Corvette, which is anchored in Dock I.

Estados Unidos

Dique II

Area in process of urbanization and construction.

Costañera Av.

Las Nereidas Fountain: It is the work of sculptor Lola Mora, who designed it in the city of Rome in 1902. Its first location was in the downtown area, but due to the scandal caused by the nude figures, it was moved to its current location in 1918. The material used is Carrara marble. Tritons, Nereids and an Aphrodite-Venus make up a harmonious sculptural work.

Museum of Telecommunications: In the 1930s, it was a beer pub built by Hungarian Modernist architect Andres Kalnay and it became a museum in 1979.

Puerto Madero, Dock III and IV

Puerto Madero Dique III y IV

If we keep walking along Puerto Madero, we will reach Docks III and IV, where the best restaurants are located. Sarmiento Frigate is anchored just a few steps from there and it is open for visitors. In the area of Docks III and IV you will see modern monumental buildings.

Once you have left Puerto Madero, you may continue walking along L. N. Alem avenue, an area where you will notice many different architectural styles. This part of the city is called El Bajo or The Downward Area. In La Recova neighborhood, which runs along L. N. Alem avenue, you will find several good-quality, inexpensive restaurants.

Telefónica de Argentina Building: This building belongs to a phone company in Argentina and it was designed by Argentinian architect César Pelli, who is famous for building lots of innovative-design structures in the United States. Its latest work is Las Petronas Towers, a building complex in Malaysia that has becomes the highest one of his kind in the whole world.

Office Building for the Department of the Army.

Argentina Postal Service Building: We suggest that you visit the halls on the ground floor and the first floor.

Dique III

The old warehouses in Puerto Madero were completely redeveloped.

Along the promenade, you will find five-star restaurants.

46

Puerto Madero

Different architectural styles on L.N. Alem avenue.

Buenos Aires Stock Exchange.

Leandro N. Alem Av.

Pt. Perón

Sarmiento

Av. Rosales

Bouchard

Corrientes Av.

Stadium

Lavalle

Plaza Roma

Tucumán

Eduardo Madero Av.

La Nación newspaper building (it is one of the most important newspapers in Spanish-speaking countries).

Dique IV

Una vista de los nuevos edificios de Puerto Madero.

47

Retiro • Plaza San Martín.

Retiro neighborhood was the location for many important historic events, the axis of which was San Martín Square. During the 18th Century, the plot of land where the square stands today used to serve as a site for slave cabins and, after that, a Bullfighting Arena for 10,000 spectators was built on the spot. In 1806, during the British Invasions, it served as scene for ferocious battles and therefore named Field of Glory. In 1812, when General San Martín arrived in Buenos Aires, it was used as a training field for the Granaderos corps, which had just been created. It was from that plot of land that the Army of the Andes departed on its mission to free Chile and Peru. The estate was finally turned into a square and named after General San Martín in 1878, for the 100th anniversary of the hero's birth.

The current landscape was designed in 1883 by French architect and landscape designer Carlos Thays. The square is on a gentle slope and on the sunny days of the year, it suddenly becomes a sunbathing spot. At the base of the slope, there stands a memorial to the soldiers that died during the war in our Malvinas (Falkland Islands) in 1982.

In the surrounding area of the square, you will find many important buildings, such as the Kavanagh (see p. 50) the Plaza Hotel, the Military Club building and San Martín Palace.

Florida street leads into the square and on its last blocks you may find many stores and shopping centers. If you walk across L.N. Alem avenue, you will reach a modern urban complex called Catalinas Norte, the most imposing group of buildings in the whole city (see p. 51). In the square's surrounding area there is a lot of cultural activity and an exciting nightlife. It is in this area that you will find the main Art Galleries in the city as well as many ethnic food restaurants and fashionable bars.

Retiro and San Martín Square in 3 Dimensions

Retiro y Plaza San Martín en 3 Dimensiones.

Military Club (Paz Palace): It was opened in 1925 and, for the time, it had a clearly academic and decadent style. It bears some resemblance with the Louvre Palace in Paris. It used to be part of a group of similar mansions that stretched along Santa Fe avenue and its surrounding area.

National Weapons Museum: It is in the same building as the Military Club, but the entrance door to the museum is at number 745, Marcelo T. de Alvear street.

Opening time: Wednesday through Friday, 3 PM to 7 PM. Admission: $ 1.

Entrance gate to the Military Club building, wrought iron and bronze.

Navy Club (see p. 52)

Pacific Galleries or "Galerías Pacífico" (see p. 52)

Catalinas Convent (see p. 52)

National Parks Service: It is one of the oldest residences that stand in the area. It was built in 1880.

Libertador Hotel.

Plaza Hotel: It is the most traditional and luxurious hotel in the city. It was designed and built by architect Zucker and it offers a great restaurant service.

Claridge Hotel.

Alas Building, on Leandro N. Alem street.

Retiro-San Martín Square

Florida street where it meets Paraguay street.

Monument to General San Martín: It stands right across Santa Fe avenue and it was the first equestrian monument in the country. It was created in 1862 by French sculptor Luis José Daumas.

Retiro Railway Station.

San Martín Palace: It is one of the seats of the Argentinian Department of State.

Kavanagh Building: It was designed in 1935 by architects Sanchez, Lagos and De La Torre. It is 120 meters high and it once was the tallest building in South America and the first one built with reinforced concrete. Its unevenly shape was a symbol of the city for a long period.

Tower of the British

Sheraton Hotel.

Monument to the arrears in the war of Malvinas in the year 1982.

Basilica of the Blessed Sacrament.

Catalinas Norte Urban Complex

51

Cultural Areas, Restaurants and Bars in Retiro, 3 Dimensions

Area cultural y gastronómica de Retiro en 3 Dimensiones.

Borges (photo by Sara Facio).

THE KILKENNY (Irish pub): M. T. de Alvear 399

BAR BARO (Meeting point for artists and intellectuals): Tres Sargentos 415

GALERÍA DEL ESTE (Bookstore, Antique Shop)

HOUSE OF BORGES: Maipú 994

FILO (Restaurant and Pizza House, Art Gallery): San Martín 975

KLEMM (Art Gallery): M. T. de Alvear 636.

DRUID (Irish pub): Reconquista 1040

CANTINA CHINA (Chinese Canteen): Maipú 967.

EL SALMON (Restaurant): Reconquista 1014

MORIZONO (Japanese Restaurant): Reconquista 899

EL VERDE (Restaurant, Bar): Reconquista 878

ICI (Institute of Iberoamerican Cooperation, Library, Auditorium and Art Gallery): Florida 943

CATALINAS (Restaurant, Lancaster Hotel): Reconquista 8?

GALERÍA DEL SOL 866.

LOTUS (Thai Food): Tres Sargentos 427

BAR DADA (Meeting point for artists and intellectuals): San Martín 943

FLORIDA GARDEN (Bar): Corner of Florida and Paraguay streets.

The area bound by San Martín Square, Santa Fé avenue, Córdoba avenue, L.N. Alem avenue and Maipú street was the core of bustling cultural activity during the 1960s, which was encouraged by numerous cultural institutions located there. The most important ones among those institutions were Di Tella Institute and, by the end of the 1970s, the CAYC (Center for Art and Communication). However, the area is also plenty of art galleries an bars which, together with these Institutions, helped create a sort of Argentinian SoHo that has only survived in part. Among the bars that were opened in those times, we can mention Bar Baro, on Tres Sargentos alley, and Florida Garden, at the corner of Florida and Paraguay streets. Both on San Martín street and on 25 de Mayo street, a group of post-modern and Irish bars and pubs have come up. They are all buzzing with activity in the evening, which creates a sophisticated and pleasant atmosphere. We suggest that you talk a walk in the area on Saturday morning and in the evening. (See pictures)

54

Retiro area-San Martín Square

Ruth Benzacar Art Gallery houses an important collection of contemporary Argentinian paintings, among which we should mention many works by Berni.

RUTH BENZACAR - Art Gallery.. Florida 1000

"Lunch", Tempera painting by Antonio Berni

"Fitz Roy Dolphin" by L.F. Benedit

"Mirrored little worm", oil painting by De La Vega

"Paradise Lost", oil painting by Luis Felipe Noé

Artists Alberto Greco, Egle Martin and Marta Minujín in Buenos Aires, 1964.

Artists Rómulo Macció, Ernesto Deira, Luis Felipe Noé and Jorge De la Vega in 1963. They led a revolutionary movement in Argentinian art in the 1960s.

55

Retiro area-San Martín Square

BUILDING OF NATIONAL PARKS. PEACE PALACE.

- Jorge Luis Borges' house
- Access to and gardens.
- Access to weapons museum of the Nation.
- Building of National Parks.
- Great rotunda.
- Peace Palace.
- Maipú
- Av. Santa Fé
- Marcelo T. de Alvear
- San Martín Square.

The Edificio de Parques Nacionales belonged to Villar and Haedo families and it was built by the architects Passeron and Brizuela by the of the 19th century in Neo-gothic style. Another building that shows a luxurious and architectonic style is the Circulo Militar that was built at the beginning of the century. It belonged to the family of Jose C. Paz, the founder of La Prensa newspaper. The building was designed by the french architect Louis Sortais. In 1938, it was acquired by the Circulo Militar. It houses the National Museum of Arms where an overview of the worldwide weapons throughout the years is shown.

ANCHORENA PALACE. Chancery.

The Palacio San Martin, where the ceremonies of the foreign affairs ministry are currently held, was the residence of Anchorena family until 1936. The plan was designed by the architect Alejandro Cristophersen for Mercedes Castellanos de Anchorena and her children. It is only one building with three independent residences connected to a central hall. The distinctive eclecticism of Christophersen can be seen here and there is a combination of elements of the French Academicism and Bourbon style. It is important to highlight the front of the new location of "Cancilleria", A "Curtain wall" seeking to have a dialogue with Palacio San Martin through the image reflected in the windows and ending in a doubtless post-modernist connection.

- San Martín Palace.
- Hall of access.
- annex expositions room
- Hall of winter.
- Arenales
- Basavilbaso
- San Martín Square.

56

Retiro-Alvear Avenue area

Retiro • Av. Alvear.

If you walk north on Esmeralda street from San Martín Square to Juncal street, you will find Estrogamou Palace (see p. 55). Arroyo street, with its art galleries and antiques shops starts there. This winding street finishes at Carlos Pellegrini Square, across 9 de Julio avenue. This little Parisian corner is surrounded by luxury houses, out of which the Brazilian and French Embassies and the Jockey Club stand out. These houses were built during the first decades of the 20th Century and they remind us of an opulent country, which at the time was called the "granary of the world".

The heads of the families who used to own these buildings were wealthy landowners in La Pampa. In building their houses, they forgot their taste for colonial architecture and gave the city a set of French-style mansions in an effort to imitate European aristocracy. Most of these buildings were designed by architects Rene Sergent, Lanus, Harry and Cristopherssen.

Retiro y Av. Alvear en 3 Dimensiones.

DUHAU RESIDENCE AND APOSTOLIC NUNCIATURE: They make up a well-matching group of 3 mansions on Alvear avenue. The Apostolic Nunciature was built by architect Le Monnier and it served as residence for popes Pius XII and John Paul II during their visits to Buenos Aires.

FRENCH EMBASSY: former Ortiz-Basualdo residence. It was built in 1912 by French architect Paul Pater.

Detail of the top floor in Lenguas Vivas School. It stands on Carlos Pellegrini avenue, across from Hyatt Hotel.

ARROYO STREET: It is one of the few winding streets in the city, which gives it a nice and singular appearance. It is crowded with art galleries and antique shops, Palatina being the most traditional one among them.

Painting by Octavio Pinto, one of the most important landscape painters in Argentina. Some of his pieces may be seen in the back hall of Palatina art gallery.

CARLOS PELLEGRINI SQUARE: Undoubtedly, it is the most French-styled square you will find in Buenos Aires. It is surrounded by a large group of examples of rationalist architecture built during the 1930s. The central area of the square is crowned by a monument to Dr Carlos Pellegrini, former Argentinian President. The Jockey Club, a prestigious institution that follows the style of the most exclusive English clubs, lies in front of the square. It has a huge and valuable library.

Retiro-Alvear Avenue area

PATIO BULLRICH: It is a classy shopping center. Inside of it, you may find some traces of the old, renovated building, which used to serve as location for livestock auctions. It has an entrance door on Posadas street and another one on Libertador avenue. In the building, there is a movie theater and some sophisticated restaurants, such as Cipriani, on Posadas street.

RESTAURANTS ON POSADAS STREET AND 9 DE JULIO AVENUE: Across from Hyatt Hotel, under the highway, the main Argentinian gourmets have opened their restaurants to offer different kinds of food to the public. The services are quite expensive. Across the street from the restaurant area, you will find Zurbarán Gallery, one of the main art galleries in the city specialized in Argentinian art.

CAESAR PALACE Hotel.

ESTRUGAMOU PALACE: It was built in 1922 by architects Sauze and Mouguier. It is a apartment building with suites covering 500 to 600 square meters. The building material was exported from France and, if you peer into the entrance hall, you will find a bronze reproduction of the Victory of Samothrace, a treasure of the Louvre in Paris.

MUSEUM OF SPANISH-AMERICAN ART "ISAAC FERNANDEZ BLANCO":

The former Nöel Palace is currently the seat for our Museum of Spanish-American Art. It was built in the 1920s by architect Martin Nöel, founder of the neocolonial architectural style. The main building, surrounded by gardens, has balconies with closings and fences in wrought iron. It houses the museum's pieces, among which we can mention a colonial silverware collection that is thought to be the most important one in the continent. The library is an interesting spot with its baroque boiserie, where valuable religious objects are on exhibition. The gardens make the perfect place to relax among the high-rise apartment buildings in the area. The Museum is located at Suipacha 1422.

Opening time: Tuesday through Sunday, 2 PM to 7 PM. Admission: $ 2.

Folkloric engraving dating from the early 19th Century period.

59

Recoleta area

La Recoleta.

In the early 18th Century, the Recoleta area used to be an impassable mount where bandits and crooks would seek refuge. The first Franciscan Chapel and Convent was built in the period ranging from 1716 to 1730 and it served as a retreat for the Order of Franciscans, who had their main church in the city's central area. These churches, located in the outskirts of the city, used to be called Recoletas and the monks who lived there were the Recoletos, which gave its name to this area of Buenos Aires.

People started to settle down in this area in 1870, when the cholera and yellow fever plagues brought wealthy families from the southern areas of the city to the north region.

The neighborhood acquired a sumptuous appearance in 1885, when Alvear avenue was built and mansions, squares and parks started to come up along it.

Behind the Church of Recoleta, there used to be an area covered with slaughterhouses and stockyards, where carts coming from the northern zones of the country would stop. It served as a meeting point for country laborers and outcasts and it was in this environment, plenty of cafeterias, general stores and tenement houses that tango music is thought to have been born. This is the place where the mythical Armenonville was located, on the corner of Libertador avenue and Tagle street. This and the Palais de Glace were the main tango ballrooms in the country.

Out tour, which comes from Alvear avenue in Retiro, will take us left to San Martín de Tours Park, a lovely place full of enormous magnolia trees. If we walk across the park to our right, we will find the cemetery, the Church of Pilar and the Recoleta Cultural Center. After that, if we walk across Francia Square, we will reach the National Museum of Fine Arts and further along a tree-covered Libertador avenue, we will find the National Library and the Museum of Decorative and Eastern Arts.

La Recoleta en 3 Dimensiones.

Building of the Car Argentine Club.

RECOLETA CEMETERY:
It is on the left side of the Church and it originally was the Convent's garden and orchard. In 1822, engineer Felipe Bertres designed the plans for a new cemetery in the northern area of the city. In 1828, Governor Manuel Dorrego made the cemetery bigger till it reached its current size. Along the cemetery's streets, you will find mausoleums with sculptures by famous local and international artists. Many well-known people are buried here, such as Eva Duarte de Perón, Domingo Faustino Sarmiento, Juan Manuel de Rosas, Facundo Quiroga and Bartolomé Mitre.

BASILICA OF OUR LADY OF PILAR: Construction began in 1716 and the church was consecrated in 1732. Its harmonious facade with pilasters and cornices is crowned by a discreet tympanum and a lateral tower that reaches 30 meters high. Inside the church you will find just one nave surrounded by niches where the smaller altars are placed. The main altarpiece was brought from northern Peru and it has a wrought-silver frontal made by Native Americans from Jujuy. The church also has a lot of interesting religious icons, such as the Christ of Humility and Patience, a Crucified Christ by sculptor Martinez Montañés, and one of the few images of San Francisco de Paola which have remained in the city.

INTENDENTE ALVEAR SQUARE:
It is located across from the Church of Pilar. If we walk across this square, we will run into Ortiz pedestrian walk, along which there are several restaurants. Going to la Biela for some coffee in the evening is a must. The hundred-year-old rubber plant in the square is the biggest one in the city. Its crown is over 70 meters wide and the tree itself is over 20 meters high. The tree's scientific name is Ficus macrophylla and it was brought from Australia. The square has recently been renovated and, during the weekend, it serves as a huge outdoors theater plenty of mimes, tango dancers and street performers.

Restaurants on Ortiz pedestrian walk, between Quintana and Guido streets.

Also in the weekend you will find a handicrafts market where you will have the opportunity to purchase pieces made by the best craftsmen at a low price.

La Biela Café, on the corner of Quintana and Ortiz streets.

Recoleta area

National Museum of Decorative and Eastern Arts (see pages 70 and 71).

National Library (see pages 68 and 69)

Pereyra Lucena

Tagle

Austria

Figueroa Alcorta Av.

Av. del Libertador

National Museum of Fine Arts (see pages 66 and 67).

Rosales

Schiaffino

Ayacucho

Recoleta Cultural Center (see pages 64 and 65)

San Martin de Tours Park, it has an area covered by magnolia trees.

Palais de Glace, exhibitions center

Statue of General Mitre, the terrace around it works as a perfect watchtower.

Monument given by the French government to the Argentinian government, located in front of the Museum of Fine Arts.

Law School, it dates from 1936 and it was built in a neoclassical German style to the likes of the military government in office at the time.

MONUMENT TO BRIGADIER GENERAL CARLOS M. DE ALVEAR: It was created by French sculptor Emile Antoine Bourdelle and it is one of the most interesting equestrian statues in the city. It was unveiled in 1925. There are many pieces by the same artist scattered around the park across the street from this monument.

"The Wounded Centaur" by Antoine Bourdelle.

"Torso" by sculptor Fernando Botero.

63

Recoleta area

Centro Cultural Recoleta en 3 Dimensiones.

Recoleta Cultural Center in 3 Dimensions.

This building was originally meant to be a Franciscan Convent and it was designed in the middle-18th Century period by Brother Blanqui. In 1858, it was enlarged and renovated by Juan Buschiazzo and, after that, it became a house for beggars and older people. The people who lived in this house were evicted in 1979 and the building became a Cultural center.

The second renovation project was undertaken by architects Clorindo Testa, Luis Benedit and Jaques Bedel.

If you walk down the entrance hall to your right, you will get to the old cloisters, which surround three patios in a row. Doing this will allow you to visit part of the original building. This area is currently devoted to exhibitions that are regularly renewed. At the end of the long corridor you will find a room where experimental theater plays are usually performed. If you walk through the patio in front of the entrance hall, you will find three special exhibition halls. One of them is called Cronopios and the other two adjoining rooms have recently been renovated, provided with equipment and conditioned. These are the halls where exhibitions by professional artists from Argentina and from abroad are usually held. There is also an auditorium right where the old chapel used to be, which was adapted to the needs of modern show halls. On the first floor, there is an interactive science museum for children. Visiting the cultural center will be an interesting experience, no matter what day of the week you do it. You will always find it buzzing with activity and shows, as well as the square in front of the entrance hall.

Behind the cultural center, you will see the Hard Rock Café, which has its entrance door on Pueyrredón avenue.

View of the O.A.S. Building

View of the exhibition halls with the original vaulted ceiling

View of the Recoleta Cultural Center facade and entrance door.

View of the old chapel (today, an auditorium).

Tank Patio.

Cistern Patio.

Exhibition Halls

Entrance stairway to the first floor.

Fountain Patio

Church of Pilar

Orange Trees Patio

Entrance door to Cronopios hall and Interactive Science Museum.

Linden Trees Patio

64

Recoleta area

If you walk along the path that is covered with trees to the right of the cultural center, you will get to a restaurant promenade where a wide range of food services is offered. Finally, if you go down on the comfortable escalator, you will enter "Buenos Aires Design", a shopping center exclusively devoted to furniture, household appliances and design objects.

Many people visit the exhibitions during the weekend.

Window to the Fountain Patio

Hard Rock Cafe Building.

"UVO" oil painting on canvass by Enzo Cuchi

View of the restaurant area

"The Wings of Desire", acrylic on canvass by Carlos Gorriarena

Entrance to Buenos Aires Design

Totem, Sculpture by Hernan Dompe

65

National Museum of Fine Arts in 3 Dimensions

Museo Nacional de Bellas Artes en 3 Dimensiones.

"Figure" by Lino Enea Spilimbergo, 1938

"Typical Orchestra" by Antonio Ber

In 1930, architect Bustillo adapted the building that used to house the water pumps of the city so that it would become the current seat for the National Museum of Fine Arts. This museum covers an area of over 10,000 square meters and it has over 10,000 works of art in its collection. It houses a permanent exhibition in which you may appreciate the most important and exhaustive collection of Argentinian sculpture and painting from the 19th and 20th Centuries. On the ground floor, you will find European paintings from every period, sculptures, paintings and tapestries from the pre-Renaissance period, the Renaissance period and the 17th, 18th and 19th Centuries. This also includes a wide range of impressionist and post-impressionist pieces.
The most important works are a series of war scenes by Goya, "The Surprised Nymph" by Manet, "The Crucifixion" by Lucas Cranach, a portrait attributed to Rembrandt, and other paintings by El Greco, Titian, Gauguin, an excellent Picasso, some works by Modigliani, Tapies, Saura, Sironi, etc.

"Processional Crucifix" anonymous in gold, bronze and crystal, 18th Century

"The Small Dove" by Ramón Gomez Cornet, 1946

Second Floor Direction, Administrat Offices and temporary exhibitions.

Segundo Pis Dirección, A ministración muestras tem porarias.

Temporary Exhibitions Wing

Primer Piso: Arte Argentino Siglo XIX, XX.
First Floor: Argentinian Art, 19th and 20th Centuries

"Secretary" by Titian Vecelli

"Landing of the Curuzú Troops" by Cándido López

"The Crucifixion of Christ" by Lucas Cranach

66

Recoleta area

Untitled, by Antonio Seguí, 1987

"On the road two" by Juan Carlos Distéfano, 1980

"The Lady of the Sea" by Paul Gauguin

"The Surprised Nymph" by Edouard Manet

"Yellow and Pink" by Edgar Degas

Temporary Exhibitions Wing

Planta Baja: Arte Europeo, prerrenacimiento Siglo XVI, XVII, XVIII, XIX, XX.

"The Kiss" by Auguste Rodin

"Portrait of Sister" by Rembrandt van Rijn

"Female Bust" by Amadeo Modigliani

Recoleta area.

Biblioteca Nacional — National Library

magnificent views of the city.
On the first underground level, you will find a valuable collection of national and local newspapers and magazines. The reading room is spacious and informal.

It is located on the plot of land of the former Presidential Residence, where its last inhabitant, Eva Perón, passed away.
Construction of the library started in the 1950s and, after many delays and difficulties, it was finally opened in 1992. The building was designed by architects Clorindo Testa, Bullrich and Cazaniga. It is situated in the center of a huge garden and it has entrance doors on Austria street and Agüero street. The building's basis is an enormous esplanade from which you can enjoy a bird's eye view of Libertador avenue and the adjoining parks.
The book storage area is located under this esplanade. It has three underground levels and it may store up to 5 million copies. An elevator will take you to the exhibition hall and the reading room, an immense suite two stories high with

Reading Room.

Map Collection.

Direction and Administrative Offices.

Elevators

Entrance Doors

Newspaper and Magazine Collections

68

Recoleta area

The old library used to be located on México street, in San Telmo quarter (see p. 27) and it was founded in 1810. Jorge Luis Borges was director of the National Library between the 1950s and the 1970s. The new library organizes a wide variety of events, both in its exhibition hall and in the auditorium it houses.

Library building as seen from Libertador avenue.

Exhibition Hall.

Jorge Luis Borges Auditorium

Esplanade

Book storage area

Across the street from the library, you will find a wide extension of parks

Recoleta area.

Museo Nacional de Arte Decorativo en 3 Dimensiones.

Facade of the museum as seen from Libertador avenue.

Wrought iron and bronze entrance gate in Louis XVI style.

"View of Rome", oil painting by Jean B. Corot

Rococo-inspired entrance door.

National Museum of Decorative and Eastern Arts in 3 Dimensions Palace Errázuriz houses the National Museum of Decorative and Eastern Arts. The project was developed by prestigious French architect Rene Sergent, who never visited Buenos Aires and yet designed most of the best mansions in the city, such as those of the Alvear family and Ernesto Bosch's. The building is designed in a French style typical of the late 18th Century period and it reminds us of the chateaux that make up the Place de la Concorde in Paris.

You may enter the museum through a wrought iron and bronze entrance gate in Louis XVI style. Once inside of the building, you will find a series of halls that have been decorated in different styles from different periods. Thus, in the first place you will find the entrance patio in Louis XVI style, then you will enter the huge reception hall in Renaissance style, a suite that has unique dimensions (20 meters long, 18 meters wide and over 10 meters high). This hall has been decorated by Nelson. Pay special attention to the magnificent fireplace and the immense windows on its sides.

Other interesting rooms in the museum are the greenhouse and the Regencia hall.

The permanent exhibition displays valuable pieces from the museum's collection, including 18th Century objects, sculptures and paintings. The museum also organizes special events and exhibitions.

Recoleta area

The countess of the Caves of Saw, oil of Anglada Camarassa.

Entrance hall decorated by Nelson. View of the magnificent fireplace carved in stone.

Louis XVI bureau and Chinese vases in Kang Hi style.

"Faint of the Virgin", Flemish carving, 15th Century.

"Virgin and Child with St John Baptist" Renaissance oil painting on wood by Jacopo dell'Sellaio

Museo de Arte Oriental

The Museum of Eastern Arts is located on the first floor of the building and it has many valuable collections of pottery, lacquerwork, engravings and furniture.

In the entrance to the museum you will find a cozy restaurant-bar with an excellent atmosphere. On the main house's basement, you will find a bookshop and souvenir store. The museum's address is Av del Libertador 1902 and it is open from Monday through Friday, 3 PM to 7 PM.

"Virgin Mary" polychrome carving, 14th Century.

Guided Tours: Wednesday through Saturday, 3 PM to 6 PM. Admission: $ 2.

Palermo Neighborhood
Palermo

In the early 17th Century, the northern area of the city was covered by lowlands and swamps that were easily flooded. A Sicilian man called Juan Palermo bought this land for agricultural purposes and he gave it the name of "Palermo Fields". It was only later, around 1820, that these premises were acquired by Rosas and annexed to the adjoining lands he already possessed. In these fields he built a huge colonial house and he surrounded it with cages that housed exotic animals, which he designed to impress and entertain his visitors. This way, he gave birth to a style that would be imitated by many South American dictators and caudillos.

In 1872, under the initiative of President Sarmiento, Tres de Febrero Park was founded. The complex was made up of a series of gardens: a zoo, a botanical garden, a rose garden and the so-called Palermo Woods, decorated with artificial lakes.

Undoubtedly, this is the greatest green area in the city and it will allow us to take a long walk in close contact with nature. There is a wide variety of trees and plants from different parts of the country, some hidden corners and gazebos next to the lakes are undoubtedly charming. We suggest you take this tour on a special sunny day and go to the Planetarium and the Sívori Museum.

Palermo area.

Palermo en 3 dimensiones - Palermo in 3 Dimensions

SÍVORI MUSEUM

It is an important museum of Argentinian painting, sculpture, engraving and illustration from the 19th and 20th Centuries. Its huge collection is only partly exhibited in this newly opened branch. Temporary exhibitions are also held in this museum. It is located at Av de la Infanta 555.

Opening time: Tuesday through Friday, 12 to 6 PM.

"The Spirit Lamp", oil painting by Marcia Schvartz.

"José León Pagano, bronce", 1936

GALILEO GALILEI PLANETARIUM: This building has a theater that sits 360 people, it is properly equipped and, on its vaulted ceiling, images of the cosmos are projected. It also serves as location for scientific events and shows. A valuable metallic meteorite is exhibited on the entrance esplanade. It fell on the province of Chaco in 1965. The Planetarium is located on the corner of Sarmiento avenue and B. Roldán street.

Opening time: Monday through Sunday, 10 AM to 6 PM. Guided Tours: Saturdays and Sundays at 3 PM, 4:30 PM and 6 PM. Admission: $ 5 for adults and $ 3 for children.

Club Gimnasia y Esgrima

Av. Infanta Isabel

Lago de Palermo

Av. Presidente Pedro Montt

Le Parc Tower: it is currently the highest building in the city.

Av. del Libertador

Paseo de la Infanta: the archways formed by the railways viaduct were nicely adapted and renovated so as to become an entertainment area where fashionable discos and restaurants create a great night life.

Residence of the US Embassy.

Plata Int. Seeber

Among the indigenous species of the Patagonic area we find the araucaria tree.

Palermo area

THE ROSE GARDENS: *You may get to the rose gardens either walking along an avenue surrounded by flowerbeds or crossing a bridge upon the lake. There are many interesting spots in the rose gardens, such as the Poet's Corner, the Andalucian Patio, the roses area and a magnificent gazebo that looks upon the lake. These gardens are plenty of visitors during the weekend.*

ZOOLOGICAL GARDEN: *The first director of the zoo was Eduardo Holmberg, a famous scientist, doctor and zoologist whose term ran from 1888 to 1904. Under his rule, the cages were designed according to the place where each animal came from. Carlos Thays finished the project in 1905. Among the dense trees and bushes we will find pagodas, Indian temples, mosques, etc. The cage that most frequently catches visitors' attention is that of the condors, which houses a cliff that was introduced in order to reproduce the high peaks of the Andes. There is also an interesting and state-of-the-art aquarium and an educational ophidians area.*

MONUMENT TO SARMIENTO: *Designed by famous French sculptor Auguste Rodin, the monument has been erected right where the house of Rosas used to stand, which is curious since he was President Sarmiento's bitterest enemy.*

MONUMENT TO THE SPANIARDS: *It is a complex sculptural work finally carved in marble. It is 25 meters high and it was erected by the city as a way to honor Spanish residents.*

75

Barrio Norte (Northern Quarter)

Barrio Norte

If we go back downtown along Callao avenue, we will find a large residential area. A row of buildings with luxurious apartments stands on both sides of the avenue up to the spot where it reaches Santa Fe avenue. There we find a commercial area with movie theaters, bars, bookstores and restaurants that, together with Corrientes avenue, makes up the right location for the busiest nightlife in the city. On Saturdays night, this area is very attractive and buzzing with activity.

If we keep on moving towards downtown on Callao avenue, we will reach Rodriguez Peña Square and, on the background, we will see Pizurno Palace, current seat of the Ministry of Education. If we turn right on Córdoba avenue and walk on block in the same direction, we will get to Aguas Corrientes Palace, a clay building that has been richly decorated. Some steps further, we will find Houssay Square, which is bounded by the Economics College Building and the Medicine College Building and Hospital, which make up the biggest construction in the city. The small church in the middle of the square used to be the chapel of the old Learning Hospital, which was located on those premises. If we walk back to Callao avenue and we keep moving along it, we will get to Corrientes avenue.

Barrio Norte en 3 dimensiones

Tympanum of the Economics College Building, on Córdoba avenue.

The Medicine College Building covers the whole block and it is the biggest construction in the city. It was built in the 1930s.

Salvador Church and School: It was built by the Jesuits and opened in 1876. The Church has three naves and it is richly decorated with Trompe o'eil paintings. The school covers the rest of the block and it is one of the most traditional Catholic schools in the city.

Some of the most beautiful domes in the city may be seen from Callao avenue. This one is located on the corner of Callao avenue and Lavalle street.

The Church of Carmen: its enormous atrium stands up to the comparatively small temple.

Clásica y Moderna is a famous restaurant-bar-bookstore in the city.

Barrio Norte (Northern Quarter)

Aguas Corrientes Palace: This gaudy building entirely decorated with English ceramic houses 12 water reservoirs, each of which can hold 70 million liters of water. Its strong outside walls are 1.80 meters thick. This palace, built in 1887, has been mentioned by Jorge Luis Borges in some of his stories, poems and essays.

Movie theaters, restaurants and bookstores area.

Rodriguez Peña Square

Several Petit Hotels are still standing in this area of the city.

Pizurno Palace: it is the current seat of the Ministry of Education. It was designed in an elegant and harmonious French style and its walls bear an original bossage.

Avenida Corrientes

Corrientes avenue is the axis of cultural life in the city of Buenos Aires. There are corners and addresses on it that make up the essence of tango, such as Corrientes 348 or the corner of Corrientes and Esmeralda street. A narrower Corrientes was, until the 1930s, the street where all tango celebrities used to gather. After the middle-1930s, it was widened and it became an avenue. It was only then that theaters and cinemas started to come up along it and it turned into the Argentinian Broadway. Undoubtedly, walking along Corrientes avenue in the evening is a must. A view of this avenue with the Obelisk on the background makes the typical postcard of Buenos Aires.
By the end of the 1950s, San Martín Theater and Cultural Center were built on Corrientes, which added another point of interest to the avenue. Theaters, cinemas, bars and libraries give it a bohemian and intellectual atmosphere. On next page, you will find a guide to the points of interest on Corrientes avenue.

Corrientes Avenue in 3 dimensions.

Av. Corrientes en 3 dimensiones

Cosmos Cinema.

Remember, jazz pub

La Casona del Teatro,

La Opera, café

La Academia: a traditional bar on the corner of Callao and Corrientes avenues.

Rojas Cultural Center: theater, bar, art gallery.

Ave Porco: disco.

Prometeo: bookstore.

El Toboso: restaurant.

La Academia: bar, café.

Zival's: books and records store.

Los Angeles: movie theater.

Pernambuco Café

Edipo: bookstore.

Bajo Corrientes: theater.

Comic Club

Píccolo: theater.

Pippo: restaurant.

Chiquilín: restaurant.

San Martín Theater

Picadilli: theater

Premier: bar, pizza house.

Politeama: bar.

Lorca: movie theater.

Hernández: bookstore

Camelot: comics store.

Lorange, movie theater

Güerrin, pi

Serafí

La Plaza: entertainment complex with theaters, bars, record stores and bookstores in a natural ambience. An excellent spot on Corrientes 1660.

Chiquilin: one of the most traditional restaurants in the city, on the corner of Montevideo and Sarmiento streets.

Pippo: restaurant specialized in pasta and beef, inexpensive. Paraná 356.

Güerrín: one of the best pizza houses in the city. Corrientes 1370

Fausto: traditional bookstore located at Corrientes 1316

Corrientes avenue is the one where you can find the highest number of bookstores in the smallest area.

Banchero: typical pizza house in Buenos Aires, on the corner of Corrientes avenue and Talcahuano street.

Corrientes Avenue

La Paz: traditional bar and restaurant that serves as meeting point for artists and intellectuals, on the corner of Corrientes avenue and Montevideo street.

- record and CD store.
- ndhi: bookstore, bar, record store, auditorium.
- Solo Cine: video club.
- Melody: record store.
- Astral: bar.
- El Gato Negro: bar.
- Presidente Alvear Theater
- Astral: theater
- La Paz: café, bar.
- Premier: movie theater (4 halls)
- Liberarte: bookstore, theater.
- Sirera: bookstore.
- El Lorraine: bookstore.
- Marin: pizza house.
- La Giralda: bar, café.
- El Foro: bar, café.
- Los Inmortales: pizza house.
- Metropolitan: theatres.
- LibroShop: bookstore.
- Ouro Preto: café, bar.
- Blanca Podestá: theater.
- Fausto: bookstore.
- Edelweiss: restaurant.
- El Vesubio: ice cream, café, restaurant.
- Gran Rex: theater.
- Tabaris: theater.
- Maipo: theater.
- Fausto: bookstore.
- Banchero: pizza house.
- Lola Membrives: theater.
- La Churrasquita: restaurant.
- Concert: theater
- La Ideal: cafeteria, bakery.
- Ópera: theater.

El Gato Negro: shop that specializes in coffee, spices and aromatic herbs. Corrientes 1669.

Liberarte: it houses a bookstore and a theater. It is sort of and off-Broadway theater. Corrientes 1555.

Gandhi: it houses a bar, a bookstore, a record store and an auditorium. It serves as meeting point for artists and intellectuals and it is one of the most interesting spots on Corrientes avenue. Corrientes 1747.

La Giralda: inexpensive and traditional bar the specialty of which is hot chocolate and fritter. Corrientes 1453.

San martín Theater and Cultural Center in 3 Dimensions.

Teatro San Martín y C. Cultural Gral. San Martín en 3 dimensiones

In 1960, the most modern and functional building of its time was opened in Buenos Aires. The huge complex had been designed by architect Mario Roberto Alvarez for the purpose of housing theaters, auditoriums, small movie projection rooms, etc.

The complex covers 29,350 square meters and both wings look clean and tidy at first sight, with enormous glass surfaces and powerful pillars that may be seen in the entrance hall.

It houses three theaters. The biggest one is called Martin Coronado and it can sit up to 1700 people. It is one of the newest and best-equipped halls in the city and its stage has witnessed the presence of the best local and international actors.

The Casacuberta theater is two stories below it, in the underground level, and it sits 560 people. It was designed as an amphitheater and it serves to put on plays that need more intimacy.

Across from the Casacuberta theater, in a spacious hall, you will find a huge mural painting 35 meters long and 11 meters high by Spanish artist Luis Seoane. It depicts theater pioneers in Argentina. On the 10th floor you will find Leopoldo Lugones hall, a small movie theater where artistic movies are usually projected. The huge entrance hall usually serves as stage for free, world-class shows in the afternoon and evening.

The San martin theater has been joined to the San martin Cultural Center on Sarmiento avenue through a passage on the ground floor, where a photographs exhibition gallery directed by prestigious photographer Sara Facio is located. In the entrance area of this gallery you will find a sculpture by Sesostris Vitullo called Martín Fierro.

The San Martin Cultural Center houses many exhibition rooms, a hall for experimental theater, an auditorium and an enormous convention hall. In the same building you will find the Tourism Department of the City of Buenos Aires, the Municipal Radio Station and a Conservatory of Music.

Municipal Radio Station.

Enrique Muiño Hall.

Sculptures Square.

Convention halls A and B.

Experimental theater hall.

"The Equilibrists", bronze sculpture by Curatella Manes. You will find it in the sculpture patio on the corner of Sarmiento and Paraná streets.

The main theater companies in the world have visited the stages of the different halls in San Martin theater.

84

Corrientes Avenue.

Teatro San Martín

San Martin Cultural Center.
Centro Cultural San Martín

View of the huge central hall on the ground floor.

Teatro San Martín
San Martin Theater.

Martín Coronado Theater hall.

Facade of San Martin theater.

Leopoldo Lugones hall, movie theater.

Offices.

Entrance Hall.

Av. Corrientes

Workshops.

Casacuberta theater hall.

Subway, Line B.

Jennifer Muller, dancer.

Oscar Araiz, choreographer.

Alfredo Alcón, actor.

Jorge Lavelli, director.

85

BER LIBER.

Lavalle Square.

Plaza Lavalle

In 1840, Mariano Miró and Felisa Dorrego bought the lands where part of the square is located today and they built a huge mansion called Miró Palace, in the gardens of which they planted a collection of trees, many of which still survive.

The mansion was demolished in 1937 in order to add those lands to the square, which thus covered the three blocks it still covers today. We suggest that you take a slow walk around the square and take your time to watch the sculptures and trees closely (see next page).

Among the buildings whose facade looks upon the square, we should mention the Federal Courthouse, Roca School, the Colon Theater, Cervantes Theater and the Sinagogue of the Israeli Congregation in Argentina, where the square meets Tucumán street. In the middle of the square you will find a column with the statue of Juan Lavalle on top of it. The square has been named after him and he was a military man educated in San Martin's army. His life was pretty violent and he was the worst enemy of Dorrego's (governor of the province of Buenos Aires), a man he later had executed by shooting. Dorrego happened to be one of Felisa Dorrego's predecessors.

Lavalle Square in 3 Dimensions.

Plaza Lavalle en 3 dimensiones

Cervantes Theater: Spanish actress María Guerrero had it built as a tribute to the city of Buenos Aires. It was opened in 1921 and, in 1961, its stage was renovated and a new wing that actually serves as workshop was added. Currently, it is the most important public theater in terms of dramatic plays. On the corner of Córdoba avenue and Libertad street, you will find the entrance door to the National Museum of Theater, where collections and documents on Argentinian theater's history are exhibited.

Opening time: Monday through Friday, 1 PM to 6:30 PM.

President Roca School: Greek-style building which has a magnificent facade with Ionic columns.

Colon Theater (see pages 90 and 91).

Agatis Robusta: Gigantic tree, 120 years old.

Sinagogue of the Israeli Congregation in Argentina: Its looks upon Libertad street. The building dates from 1932 and it is one of the main synagogues in the city.

Massüe Mirador: It is one of the few examples of Art Nouveau architecture in the city.

Jujuy's Ceibo Tree: Historic tree that was planted in 1878.

Lavalle Square.

Obelisk: It was built in the 1930s by architect Prebich. It stands there to commemorate the place where the Argentinian flag was hoisted for the first time. The Church of St Nicholas used to be located on these plot of land and it was later moved to Santa Fe avenue, between Talcahuano and Uruguay streets.

Obelisco

Av. Corrientes

Diagonal Norte

Lavalle

Monumento a las victimas de la AMIA

Talcahuano

Ficus macrophyllia: A tree whose trunk is over 80 meters in diameter.

Artists Tenement House: This building is located at Libertad 543. It dates from 1907 and it has served as the house for many artists' workshops since 1966.

Edelweiss Restaurant: it is the traditional place to go for dinner after a show in the Colon Theater.

Federal Courthouse: It is the seat of the judicial body. The project was designed by architect Norberto Maillard and construction began in 1889 but it only finished in 1942, after many disputes had taken place. It is an eclectic building and, undoubtedly, its monumental sense of esthetics is pretty questionable.

Second-hand books market.

Statue of Juan Lavalle.

89

Lavalle Square.

Teatro Colón en 3 dimensiones   Colon Theater in 3D

Facade of Colon Theater on Libertad street.

The first building for the Colon Theater was located on Av de Mayo, where the National Bank stands today. By the end of the 19th Century, Buenos Aires had become a wealthy city and the theater was not as luxurious as the new generations wanted it to be, so the project for a new Colon Theater was designed. The original plans were drawn by Italian architect Francisco Tamburini and submitted for approval in 1829. The theater was to be located in front of Lavalle Square. After a series of never-ending difficulties, architect Julio Dormal finally finished it in 1908. The main theater has a seating capacity of 2,500 and it may accommodate up to 3,500 people if standing tickets are sold. The main entrance door to the orchestra floor and boxes is on Libertad street and the higher seating rows in the theater may be entered though the entrance doors on Toscanini and Tucumán streets.

The main hall is enormous and it is entirely covered in stucco that has been molded by Italian artisans. There is a combination of styles that may be appreciated by seeing the Ionic and Corinthian capitals. On the ceiling, there is a French stained-glass piece. The main staircase leading to the theater itself is made up of a combination of Carrara marbles from Verona and Portugal. The banister's tops are craved by a famous sculptor

called Chapasco. In this hall you will find a small museum of history of the Colon Theater and a museum of old and valuable musical instruments. There is also a public library that has books on music and opera. If you go up any of the lateral stairs, you will get to the hall of Busts, a long wide corridor where you will find the faces of the most famous musicians of all times on the lintels. One of the lateral walks will take you to the Golden Hall, an exquisitely decorated room with gilded details and French furniture, chandeliers and vases.

The main theater has an Italian-style horseshoe design, there are three stories with boxes on balconies, then a gallery for women, an upper gallery, another gallery above it and finally a paradise or top gallery. The theater is 33 meters in diameter and 28 meters high. The dome's ceiling was painted by famous artist Raúl Soldi. The main chandelier is a unique piece with more than 600 light bulbs. It weighs 2,500 kilos and a maximum of 20 people can stand inside of it to create sound effects during the show.

Stage.

Performer's entrance door.

Calle Cerrito

Costume designers workshop.

Shoe designers workshop.

Hairdresser's.

Technical Office.

Stage designers workshop.

View of the canopy built on the entrance door after the opening.

Lavalle Square

Main theater.

White Hall.

Golden Hall.

Facade on Toscanini street. Italian-style pilasters and bas-reliefs.

Calle Libertad

View of the upper galleries as seen from the entrance hall.

Arturo Toscanini

Main Hall.

Hall of Busts.

Storage rooms.

Entrance for visitors. Guided tours: Monday through Friday: 9 AM, 10 AM, 11 AM, 12 AM, 1 PM, 2 PM, 3 PM and 4 PM. Saturdays: : 9 AM, 10 AM, 11 AM and 12 AM. Admission: $ 5. Toscanini street 1180. Information: 4382-6632.

Balconies with caryatids on the facade upon Libertad street.

Sculpture workshop.

Machinery and carpenter's workshop.

Theater with dome's ceiling painted by Raúl Soldi and main chandelier with over 600 light bulbs.

Stage designers workshop on the third underground level.

Colon Theater: Its Workshops and Companies.

Teatro Colón, talleres y cuerpos artísticos

The theater's workshops are located in the underground levels. It is one of the few opera houses in the world in which most of the articles needed for the show may be produced. It has a stage designers workshop, a hairdresser's, a shoemaking workshop, a costume design workshop, a carpenter's workshop, etc.
Quite an army of people work in these underground levels, which stretch below Viamonte street and 9 de Julio avenue.
The Colon Theater has its own art companies: a Philharmonic Orchestra, a Choir and a Ballet Company. There are over one hundred company members in all.

The main opera and ballet starts in the world have set foot on the theater's stage, among them we can mention: Lili Pons, Enrique Caruso, María Callas and Luciano Pavarotti (the most famous opera singers in this century) as well as Rudolf Nureyev and Nijinsky (the main ballet dancers). Julio Boca, Maximiliano Herrera and Paloma Herrera, the most important ballet dancers from Argentina, were educated in the Colon Theater's school.
Among musicians and conductors, we should mention the performance of Richard Strauss in 1920, as well as the concerts given by Igor Stravinsky and the unforgettable shows of Pablo Casals and Manuel de Falla. Arturo Toscanini conducted the theater's orchestra in many opportunities and it is in his honor that one of the lateral streets of the theater has been called Toscanini.
The list of famous performers is never-ending, but we could also mention the Vienna Boys' Choir, Alfredo Kraus, José Carreras, Plácido Domingo, Herbert Von Karajian, Maurice Bejart, Margot Fontaine, Maia Plissetskaya, etc.

Sculpture storage room on the third underground level.

Scene of Les Sylphides.

Marcia Haydee and the Stuttgart Ballet.

Astor Piazzolla: he gave his consecrating concert in the theater.

Richard Strauss conducted in the Colon Theater during his two visits to Buenos Aires.

Beniamino Gigli performed in the theater many seasons.

Mascagni conducted his Cavalleria rusticana in 1911.

Congress Square and Great Domes.

Plaza Congreso y las grandes Cúpulas.

Congress Square and Great Domes
Avenida de Mayo stretches from Plaza de Mayo to Congress Square, which is framed by several rows of magnificent buildings with domes in a great variety of styles. The most outstanding ones are the Barolo building, the Inmobiliaria building, the Urban Heritage building, the Molino building and the National Congress building.
Congress Square was created to commemorate the centennial of the May Revolution in 1910 and it was designed as a monumental frame for the Congress building, which had been opened in 1906.
In the square, the Fountain of the Two Congresses stands out with its huge staircases and banisters. At dusk, the combination of water, music and lights makes up a nice show.
On the corner of Bartolomé Mitre and Paraná streets you will find the Church of la Piedad, a spacious example of neoclassical architecture. That block on Bartolomé Mitre street is another one among the many Parisian corners in the city. In La piedad Passage you will find restaurants and nightclubs.

Congress Square in 3 Dimensions

Plaza Congreso en 3 dimensiones

BAROLO BUILDING: It dates from 1922 and it was designed by Italian architect Mario Palanti. For a period, it was the highest building in Buenos Aires. A rare example of expressionist architecture, it has a monumental appearance and a spacious gallery that reaches Hipólito Irigoyen street. Even though this gallery is somehow deteriorated, it is still faithful to its original appearance. If you take a close look at the building, you will find some hidden esoteric details included by architect Palanti, such as the gargoyles, the dragons, the circles and the balustrades that may be seen in the main vault. The number and measures of these elements have been taken from figures and keys provided by Dante in The Divine Comedy.

Former building of the Spanish Association of Mutual Aid and current annex to the Congress building for the Senate.

Main body of the Monument to the Two Congresses

INMOBILIARIA BUILDING: It was built by an insurance company called La Inmobiliaria in 1910. It is a mixture of styles. The lower floors, with archways, statues and balconies have an evident Italian style, whereas the two domes on the corners give it an original and exotic Eastern style.

The area is full of cafés and bars with tables on the sidewalk, and there are also some theaters and nightclubs. The most important theater among them is Avenida Theater, a traditional house where zarzuelas (Spanish form of light opera) are usually performed. A group of excellent Spanish restaurants surrounds the theater. Across the street from the square, on Rivadavia street, you will see Liceo Theater, a traditional old little theater.
The Avila Bar on Av de Mayo 1300 and Agua y Fuego on Rivadavia 1400 are nice places to have dinner in and enjoy Flamenco shows at the same time.

Avenida Theater (Av de Mayo 1222): it was recently restored after a fire. It is one of the most important and traditional theaters for light opera.

Congreso Square

View of the square with the Congress in the background.

National Congress (see pages 96 and 97)

Av. Callao

Av. Rivadavia

Dome of the former Molino Café

Edificio del patrimonio urbano

Montevideo

Paraná

Bartolomé Mitre

La Piedad Passage: Charming spot in the city built as a condominium at the beginning of this Century. It has gone through terrible deterioration and mutilations over the years, but its charm is still intact. The outside street has a nice Parisian touch and the narrow inside passages remind us of some places in Rome.

Statue to the Thinking man by Auguste Rodin.

Former Majestic Hotel: It serves as headquarters for a government office nowadays but it used to be one of the main hotels in the city. Its robust frame has a square dome on top of it. This is the place where Nijinsky resided during his stay in Buenos Aires.

La Piedad Church: This church was designed in a typical neoclassical style with a huge central nave and a high dome. The church is richly decorated on the inside and it has icons that date from the 18th Century.

El Congreso Nacional en 3 dimensiones

Under a law enacted in 1889, the National Congress was moved to the lands of an old sawmill on the block bound by Callao street, Hipólito Irigoyen street, Pozos street and Rivadavia avenue.
In 1896, once Av de Mayo had been finished, the government opened an international bidding for the building's construction works. As a result of this process, construction of the building was left in the hands of architect Victor Meano, who had been working in the country for a while and helping architect Tamburini in the Colon Theater project and other buildings.

The National Congress is a monumental building in a classic Greek-Latin style. It may be viewed properly from Av de Mayo, which makes up an axis with the Executive Office Building or Pink House on one end and the National Congress, which houses the legislative body, on the other one. The National Congress was opened in 1906 and the buildings that surround it were finished in 1910, for the Independence Centennial celebrations. Its decoration is made up of a combination of marble and granite, which gathers both Roman monumentality and Greek austerity.

The huge central dome of the legislative body: the Chamber of Representatives covers the back central area of the building and its semicircular shape may be seen from Pozos street, whereas the Chamber of Senators is located in the left wing of the building and it is quite smaller.
Undoubtedly, the most magnificent spot in the building is the Blue Hall, which lies under the big dome (approx. 60 meters high). The ceiling bears some beautiful marble cravings, some allegoric statues

Chamber of Representatives
Hall of the Lost Paces
Blue Hall
Pink Hall
Chamber of Senators

National Congress building is meant to remind us of its sister in Washington. The building bears some perfectly carved caryatids, quadrigas and capitals you should not miss. Inside of it, there is a series of beautiful halls and a library with a wide range of valuable and out of print books. It houses the two chambers that make up Argentina's and a 2-ton chandelier made up of bronze and Baccarat crystal. This is the place where the exequies of the most important political figures in the country are usually held. Nowadays, the building is not big enough to house all the Congress staff and that is the reason why many of the surrounding buildings serve as annexes to it.

Congreso Square

View of the Congress as seen from Av de Mayo.

Caryatids at the National Congress' side doors.

Av. Callao

Reading Hall for the Chamber of Senators.

Big Hall.

Library.

Greek-Roman style decoration.

El Abasto en 3 dimensiones

In 1890, a foodstuffs market called Abasto was erected on Corrientes avenue. Some time later, a new neighborhood started to grow around it and it took the market's name. In 1931, construction works began for a new market building in modernist Art-decó style with big domes in reinforced concrete. In the early 20th Century, when the first market was built, the area took a different shape thanks to the presence of carriages, laborers, hostels and canteens which gave it a marginal ambience where tango music, popular songs and people's poetry were easily spread. One of the most important tango figures that lived in the area was Carlos Gardel, the city's mythical singer. Today, a street and a subway station that carry his name remind us of his presence in the neighborhood. The area is taking new shape again now: high-rise apartment buildings, five-star hotels, night clubs and theaters are being built and the old market has become a giant shopping mall.

View of the old market in the 1930s.

Babilonia: restaurant and theater that offers high-quality shows.

Detail of the monumental archways.

Facade of the former Abasto market on Corrientes avenue.

Interior of the restored building where a giant shopping mall stands today.

Tango

The origins of tango music date back to the period that stretches from the 1850s to the 1880s. Tango music is deeply influenced by African-American rhythms, such as candombe and habanera, and by some European dances, such as Spanish contredanse and the so-called Andalusian tango. Those are the predecessors of Argentinian tango.

In the late 19th Century, the so-called suburban tango became consolidated. At the beginning, people used to dance the tango in the suburbs and it was not until the early 20th Century that it was accepted as a decent dance in luxurious downtown dance halls.

Tango music later took its strength of character and melancholy cadence from the mainly Italian and Spanish immigrants that arrived in the city at the begining of this Century. Around 1910, tango music had already spread to Europe and it was widely accepted in all the big cities in the world, whereas in Buenos Aires it still aroused suspicion, specially among members of the Catholic Church, who even condemned it.

Hansen's, the Armenonville and Chanteclair were the places where this dance was first accepted and their customers quickly became fans of it. Dance parties and meetings started to spread all around the city at a fast pace and thus appeared the greatest tango composers, performers, dancers and writers in the city. At this stage, the bandoneon became the main musical instrument in Typical Orchestras, that is, tango orchestras created by Vicente Greco.

In the 1920s, tango music became worldwide famous and Buenos Aires, which was enjoying good economical conditions at the time, show itself as the Queen of the River Plate.

Its nightlife gained fame together with Corrientes street (which had not become an avenue yet) and it huge cabarets. This situation lead tango music to its golden period.

The most important figure in tango music is Carlos Gardel, a mythical singer born in France and raised in the Abasto market neighborhood who possessed a great deal of magnetism and a privileged voice.

Corrientes street before it became an avenue.

Vicente Greco

Carlos Gardel with the so-called New York Blondes: he embodies the myth of the Argentine winner who attains success in Hollywood.

99

Tango

Carlos Gardel was responsible for taking tango music to Broadway and Hollywood. Agustin Bardi, Julio Decaro, Celedonio Flores, Discépolo, Osvaldo Fresedo, Osvaldo Pugliese and Aníbal Troilo were the main tango composers and performers in Argentina. In the 1920-1950 period several tango schools were created: some of them supported sung tango and focused on the poetics of the lyrics, whereas others, such as that of Anibal Troilo or Osvaldo Pugliese, supported the dance side of tango. Among great tango singers we should mention Julio Sosa, Edmundo Rivero, Roberto Goyeneche, Libertad Lamarque and Hugo del Carril. Tango lyrics writers were great poets, as is the case with Homero Manzi, Horacio Ferrer, and even Jorge Luis Borges himself, who did not miss the chance to write the lyrics of some famous tango songs.

Astor Piazzolla, a musician and disciple of Anibal Troilo, was also the last great innovator in tango music. He placed tango music closer to contemporary music and was widely accepted and acknowledged as one of the greatest composers of these times.

Nowadays, thousands of tourist arrive in Buenos Aires with a main goal: watching tango shows and learning how to dance to the beat of this fascinating music that is, as a great poet once said, "a sad feeling you can dance to".

Typical Orchestra with a bandoneon as the main instrument.

Julio Sosa, Tango singer.

Osvaldo Fresedo, composer.

Aníbal Troilo a.k.a. "Pichuco", the greatest bandoneon player and tango composer in the world.

Roberto Goyeneche, tango singer.

Homero Manzi, lyrics writer and poet.

100

Tango

Eyewitness Travelguide to Buenos Aires

GALERÍAS DE ARTE
De Santi: M.T.de Alvear 868
Der Brücke : Paseo de la Infanta, Arco N° 10.
El Socorro: Suipacha 1331
Gal.Museo Aguilar: Suipacha 1178
Klemm: M.T. de Alvear 636
Lagard: Suipacha 1216
Le Point: Suipacha 1250
Leonardo Avalos: Arroyo 858
Palatina: Arroyo 821
Praxis Arte Internacional: Arenales 1311
Rubbers: Suipacha 1175
Ruth Benzacar: Florida 1000
Artistas Plásticos: Viamonte 458
Suipacha: Suipacha 1248
Van Eyck: Sta.Fe 834
Van Riel: Talcahuano 1257
Vermeer Galería de Arte: Suipacha 1168
VyP: Arroyo 971
Zurbarán: Cerrito 1522
Espacio Giesso: Defensa 1326
Sara García Uriburu: Uruguay 1223
Art House: Uruguay 1223

MUSEOS
Museo Hispanoamericano: Suipacha 1422
Museo de Arte Decorativo: Av. del Libertador 1900
Museo de Arte Moderno: San Juan 350
Museo de Arte Oriental: Av. Libertador 1902
Museo Nacional de Bellas Artes: Av. del Libertador 1473
Museo Eduardo Sívori: Av. Infanta Isabel 555
Museo Xul Solar: Laprida 1212
Salón de Exposiciones Palais de Glace: Posadas 1725

CINES
Alto Palermo: Av. Santa Fe 3235 - 827-8362
Ambasador: Lavalle 777 - 322-9700
América: Callao 1057 - 811-3818
Atlas Belgrano: Av. Cabildo 2165 - 781-7200
Atlas Lavalle: Lavalle 869 - 322-1936
Atlas Recoleta: Guido 1952 - 803-3313
Atlas Santa Fe: Av. Santa Fe 2015 - 823-7878
Auditorio Maxi: Carlos Pellegrini 657 - 326-1822
Belgrano Multiplex: Obligado y Mendoza: 781-8183
Capitol: Av. Santa Fe 1848 - 812-2379
Cineplex: Lavalle 727 - 393-8610
Complejo Tita Merello: Suipacha 442 - 322-1195
Electric Lavalle: Lavalle 836 - 322-1846
Galerías Pacífico: Florida 735 - 319-5357
Gamount: Rivadavia 1635 - 371-3050
General Paz: Av. Cabildo 2702 - 781-1412
Grand Splendid: Av. Santa Fe 1860 - 812-0808
Leopoldo Lugones: Av. Corrientes 1530 - 374-8611
Lorange: Av. Corrientes 1372 - 373-2411
Lorca: Av. Corrientes 1428 - 371-5017
Los Angeles: Av. Corrients 177/70 - 371-3742
Losuar: Av. Corrientes 1743 - 371-6100
Maxi 1-2-3: C.Pellegrini 657 - 326-1822
Metro: Cerrito 570 - 382-4219
Monumental: Lavalle 780 - 393-8865
Normandie: Lavalle 855 - 322-1000
Ocean: Lavalle 739 - 322-1515
Paseo Alcorta: Av. F. Alcorta y Salguero: 806-5665
Patio Bullrich: Av. Libertador 750 - 815-8328

Premier: Av. Corrientes 1565 - 374-2113
Santa Fe: Av. Santa Fe 1947 - 812-8980
Savoy: Av. Cabildo 2829 - 781-9400
Solar de la Abadía: Luis M. Campos y Maure - 778-5181
Trocadero: Lavalle 820 - 393-8321.

TEATROS
Astral: Av. Corrientes 1639 - 374-5707
Ateneo: Paraguay 918 - 328-2888
Avenida: Av. de Mayo 1222 - 381-0662
Blanca Podestá: Av. Corrientes 1283 - 382-2592
Broadway: Av. Corrientes 1155 - 382-2345
Cátulo Castillo: Bmé. Mitre 970 - 345-2774
Cervantes: Libertad 815 - 816-4224
Colón: Libertad 621 - 382-5414
Del Centro: Sarmiento 1249 - 417-7097
Del Globo: M.T. de Alvear 1155 - 816-3307
Del Pueblo: Diag. Norte 943 - 326-3606
Del Sur: Venezuela 1286 - 383-5702
El Excéntrico: Lerma 47
Empire: H.l Yrigoyen 1934 - 953-8254
General San Martín: Av. Corrientes 1530 - 371-0118
Gran Rex: Corrientes 900 - 322-8000
La Plaza: Av. Corrientes 1660 - 371-7623
La Trastienda: Balcarce 460 - 342-7650
Liberarte: Av. Corrientes 1555 - 375-2341
Liceo: Rivadavia y Paraná - 381-4291
Lola Membrives: Av. Corrientes 1280 - 383-2025
Maipo: Esmeralda 433 - 322-4882
Manzana de las Luces: Perú 294 - 342-9930
Margarita Xirgu : Chacabuco 875 - 300-2448
Metropolitan: Av. Corrientes 1343 - 371-0816
Off Corrientes: Av. Corrientes 1632 - 373-3608
Opera: Corrientes 900 - 326-1335
Payró: San Martín 766 - 312-5922
Picadilly Teatro: Av. Corrientes 1254 - 373-1900
Piccolo Teatro: Av. Corrientes 1624 - 373-3465
Presidente Alvear: Av. Corrientes 1659 - 374-6076
Megafón: Chacabuco 1072.

SHOPPINGS
Alto Palermo: Av. Santa Fe 3251
Galerías Pacífico: Florida 753
Paseo Alcorta: Salguero y Av. Figueroa Alcorta
Patio Bullrich: Av. del Libertador 250
Abasto: Corrientes entre Agüero y Anchorena
Spinetto: Moreno y Alberti

HOTELES ★★★★★
Alvear Palace H.: Av. Alvear 1891 - 804-4031
Caesar Park Buenos Aires - Posadas 1232 - 814-5150
H. Etoile: Pte. R.M. Ortiz 1835 - 804.-8603
Bahuen: Av. Callao 346 - 804-1600
Claridge: Tucumán 535 - 314-7700
Libertador Kemplinsky Buenos Aires: Av. Córdoba y Maipú - 322-2095
H. Panamericano: C. Pellegrini - 393-6017
Marriot Plaza: Florida 1005 - 318-3000
Park Hyatt Buenos Aires: Posadas 1088 - 326-1234
Sheraton Buenos Aires & Towers: San Martín 1225 - 311-6311.
Hotel Intercontinental: Moreno 809 - 340-7100

HOTELES ★★★★
Ap H. Las Naciones: Av. Corrientes 818 - 325-2491
Ap H. Benco: H.Yrigoyen 1534 - 476-1192
Ap H. Arenales: Arenales 855 - 322-7196
Ap H Bauen Suite: Av. Corrientes 1856 - 804-1600
Ap H. Esmeralda: M.T. de Alvear 842 - 311-7632
Ap H. Obelisco Center: Pte. Roque S. Peña 991 - 382-9100
Ap H. Plaza San Martín: Suipacha 1092 - 312-4767
Ap H. Recoleta: Guido 1948 - 803-2397
Ap H. Suipacha: Suipacha 1235 - 393-3088
Ap Ulises Recoleta: Ayacucho 2016 - 803-4457
Bisonte: Paraguay 1207 - 394-8041
Bisonte Palace: M.T. de Alvear 902 - 311-4751
Carlton: Libertad 1180 - 812-0081
Gran Hotel Buenos Aires: Alvear 797 - 312-3003
Gran Hotel Colón: Carlos Pellegrini 507 - 325-1017
Gran Hotel King: Lavalle 560 . 393-4012
Bristol: Cerrito 286 - 382-5401
Carsson: Viamonte 650 -322-3551
Castelar: Av. de Mayo 1152 - 383-5000
Hotel Continental: Av. R.S.Saenz 725 - 326-3250
Crillon: Av. Santa Fe 796 - 312-8181
De las Américas: Libertad 1020 - 393-3432
Hotel Dorá: Maipú 963 - 312-7391
Hotel El Conquistador: Suipacha 948 - 328-3012
La Fayette: Reconquista 546 - 393-9081
Lancaster: Córdoba 405 - 311-3021
Nogaró: Diag. J.A. Roca 562 .-331-0991
Posta Carretas: Esmeralda 726 - 394-1625
Presidente: Cerrito 846 - 372-5081
Recoleta Plaza: Posadas 1557 - 804-3471
Regidor: Tucumán 451 - 314-7917
República: Cerrito 370 - 382-4011
Rochester: Esmeralda 542 - 326-6076
Salles: Cerrito 208 - 382-0091
Savoy: Callao 181 - 372-7788

HOTELES ★★★
Benco: H. Yrigoyen 1534 - 476-1192
Camino Real: Maipú 572 - 392-3162
City: Bolivar 160 - 383-6481
Embajador: C. Pellegrini 1181 - 393-9485
Gran Argentino: C. Pellegrini 37 - 345-3073
Gran Eibar: Florida 328 - 325-1698
Orly: Paraguay 474 - 312.4344
San Carlos: Suipacha 39 - 345-1022
Ap. Embassy: Av. Córdoba 860 - 322-1228
Columbia Palace: Corrientes 1533 - 373.-2123
Concord: 25 de Mayo 630 - 313-2018
Constitución Palace: Lima 1696 - 305-9011
Hotel Deauville: Talcahuano 1253- 812-1560
Eleven Palace: La Rioja 87 - 864-5097
Esmeralda Palace: Esmeralda 52 - 393-1085
Impala: Libertad 1215 - 812-5696
Italia Romanelli: Reconquista 647 - 312-6361
Liberty: Corrientes 632 - 325-0261
Monumental: Junín 357 - 953-8472
Napoleón: Rivadavia 1364 - 383-2031
Normandie: R. Peña 320 - 374-7001
Plaza Francia: Pje. Schiaffino 2189 - 804-9631
Promenade: M.T. de Alvear 444 - 312-5681
Victory: Maipú 880 - 322-8415
Waldorf: Paraguay 450 - 312-2071

WHERE TO EAT.

LA BOCA

Caminito Tango Show
Del Valle Iberlucea 1151
Te. 4301-1520/30
Cocina internacional / International cuisine

Campo e Mare
Lamadrid 701 Tel. 4302-0785
Parrilla / Argentine barbecue

Cantina Gennarino
Necochea 1210 Tel. 4301-6617
Cocina Italiana / Seafood

El Obrero
Cafarena 64 Tel. 4362-9912
Cocina Argentina / Argentine cuisine

El Puentecito
Luján 2101 Tel. 4301-1794
Parrila / Argentine cuisine

La Barbería
Av. Pedro de Mendoza 19598
Tel. 4301-8870
Pescados y mariscos / Seafood

Il Matterello
Martín Rodríguez 517 tel. 4307-0529
Cocina italiana / Italian cuisine

Il Piccolo Vapore
Necochea 1190 Tel. 4301-4455
Cocina Italiana / Italian Cusine

La Ribera
Av. Pedro de Mendoza 1875
Tel. 4301-5160

La Cancha
Brandsen 697 Tel. 4362-2975
Pescados y Mariscos / Seafood

Valle de Palos
Aristóbulo del Valle 600
Tel. 4300-0671
Cocina Casera / Home made cuisine

Viejo Puente de Mario
Av. Alte. Brown 1499 Tel. 4301-2170
Pescados y mariscos / Seafodd

SAN TELMO • MONTSERRAT.

Asociación Sueca
Tacuarí 147 Tel. 4334-7813/9552
Cocina Sueca / Swedish Cuisine

Ban/Juu
México 1424 Tel. 4381-1259
Cocina Japonesa / Japanese cusine

Bidou de las Luces
Perú 269 Tel. 4801- 1844
Cicina Argentina / Argentine cuisine

Basque Francés
Moreno 1370
Tel. 4382-0244 / 383-5021
Cocina Vasco francés/ Basque cuisine

Campo dei Fiori
San José 491 Tel. 4381-1800/8402
Cocina italiana / Italian cuisine

Centro Asturiano
Solís 475 Tel. 4381-1342
Cocina española / Spanish cuisine

Como en casa
H. Yrigoyen 1315 Tel. 4383-2865
Cocina Argentina / Argentine cuisine

El acuerdo
Moreno 360 Tel. 4331-4172

El Caserío
H. yrigoyen 575 tel. 4331-1336

El Globo
H. Yrigoyen 1199 Tel. 381-3926
Cocina española / Spanish cuisine

El Querandí
Perú 302 Tel. 4345-0331/ 1770
Cocina Argentina / Argentine cuisine

El Rocío
Salta 151 tel. 4381-7502
Cocina Internacional / International cuisine

La María
México 1310 tel. 4383-0173
Pastas

La Posada de Don Quijote
Lima 387 Tel. 4383-8602
Cocina internacional / International cuisine

La Tasca
H. Yrigoyen 1218 tel. 4381-1290

Mesón Español
H. Yrigoyen 1211 1° tel. 4384-6667
Cocina Española / Spanish cuisine

Morocco
H. Yrigoyen 851 Tel. 4342-6046
Cocina exótica / Exotic cuisine

New Shushina
Solís 275 Tel. 4372-1056
Cocina Japonesa / Japanese cuisine

Plaza Mayor
Venezuela 1399 tel. 4383-0788
Cocina Española / Spanish cuisine

Prosciutto
Venezuela 1212 Tel. 4383-8058
Cocina Italiana / italian cuisine

Rivero al Sur
Luis Saenz peña Esq. Estados Unidos
Cena Show / Dinner show

Status
Virrey Ceballos 178
Tel. 4372- 6282 / 382-8531

Argentina is well-known as a country for the quality of its beef. In the so-called "parrillas" (grills) you will be able to try different cuts, such as tenderloin, t-bones, ribs, etc.

Eyewitness Travelguide to Buenos Aires

Vieja Victoria
H. Yrigoyen 778
Tel. 4372-6282 /4316
Parrila / Argentine barbecue

PALERMO • LAS CAÑITAS

Almacén Cabrera
Cabrera 4399 Tel. 4832-4670
Cocina Criolla / Native cuisine

Al Shark
Av. Scalabrini Ortiz 1550
Tel. 4833-2049/6933
Cocina Arabe / Arabian cuisine

Azafrán
Honduras 5143 Tel. 4832-6487
Cocina casera / Home made cuisine

Bella Italia
Rep. Arabe Siria 3285
Tel. 4802-4253
Cocina Italiana / Italian cuisine

Buenos Aires News
Paseo de la Infanta
Av. Del Libertador y Av. De la Infanta
Tel. 4778-1500 / 0127
Cocina Internacional / internationale cuisine

Cala
Soler 4065 Tel.4823-0413
Cocina Francesa / french cuisine

Campo Alto
Arenales 3360 Tel. 4821-6030 /6059
Cocina Argentina / Argentine cuisine

Cangas de Narcea
Av. Godoy Cruz 3108
Tel. 4773-4601 / 6706
Cocina Internacional / International cuisine

Casona María María
Güemez 3140 Tel. 4821-3817
Cocina italiana / Italian cuisine

Centro de la Olla
Jorge Luis Borges 1559
Pizza y Pasta

Cielito Lindo
El Salvador 4999 Tel. 4832-8054
Cocina Mexicana / mexican cuisine

Club del Golf
Av. Tornquist 6385
Tel. 4775-0148 / 0197
Cocina Internacional / International cuisine

Cosa Nostra
Cabrera 4270 tel. 4862-1906
Cocina Italiana / italian cuisine

Cristophe
Fitz Roy 1994 Tel. 4771-1155
Cocina Francesa / French cuisine

Del Tomate
Salguero 2963 Tel. 4804-7882
Pastas

Dimitri. Puente Mitre
Av. Caseros y vías del ferrocarril
Tel. 4806-0022
Cena Show / dinner show

Dolli .Av. Figueroa Alcorta 3004
Tel. 4806-3366 / 3257
Cocina Internacional / International cuisine

Domani
Salguero 3000 Tel. 4807-5288
Pizza y pasta

Don Battaglia
Av. Scalabrini Ortiz 803
Tel. 4773-0484 / 0597
Cocina Argentina / Argentine cuisine

Doney
Av. Del Libertador 3096
Tel. 4802-0075
Minutas / Fast Food

El Beduino
Av. Scalabrini Ortiz 1453
Tel. 4831-6951
Cocina Internacional / International cuisine

El Lugar de Angel
Av. Del Libertador 4534
Tel. 4771-3179
Cocina Internacional / Internatiional cuisine

El Oso del Charlie
Av. Del Libertador 4534
Tel. 4771-9184
Cocina Internacional / International cuisine

El Sheik
Rep. Arabe Siria 3330 Tel. 4806-1398
Cocina Arabe / Arabian cuisine

El Taller
Honduras 4988 Tel. 4831-5501
Minutas / Fast food

Beckett bar, restaurant, galeria de arte.
El Salvador 4960. Tel. 4831-7373

El Trapiche
Paraguay 5099 Tel. 4772-7343
Cocina Internacional / International cuisine

Gascón
Av. Córdoba y Gascón
Tel. 4862-9662
Cocina Internacional / International cuisine

Gitana Bs. As. News
Paseo de la Infanta
Av. Del Libertador Tel. 4778-1500
Cocina Española / Spanish cuisine

Guido's
Rep. De la India 2843 Tel. 4802-2391
Pastas

Habano
Seguí 4674 Tel. 4777-|043
Cocina Internacional / International cuisine

Hermann
Av. Santa Fe 3902 Tel. 4382-1929
Cocina Alemana / German cuisine

Incontro
Guatemala 5602 tel. 4775-7016
Cocina Italiana / Italian cuisine

Lusef
Malabia 1378 Tel. 4773-0450
Cocina Siria / Ssyrian cuisine

Jade
Ugarteche 3033
 tel. 4803-2838
Cocina china / Chinese cuisine

Kalaat Yandal
Malabia 1467
Tel. 4831-1587
Cocina Arabe / Arabian cuisine

Katmandú
Av. Córdoba 3447
Tel. 4963-1122 / 3250
Cocina Huindú / Hindu cuisine

Kisher's
Av Cordoba 4660 tel. 4773-1888
Cocina Judía / Jewish cuisine

La Boguedita
Gascón 1460 Tel. 4867-1619
Cocina Cubana / Cuban cuisine

La Canzonetta
Av. Dorrego 1556 Tel. 4771-3998
Cocina Italiana / Italian cuisine

La Capillita
Av. Dorrego 2898 Tel. 4778-0068
Pescados y Mariscos / Seafood

La Casa Polaca
Jorge Luis Borges 2076
Tel. 4774-7621
Cocina Polaca / Polish cuisine

La Copa de Oro de Carlitos
Olleros 1667 Tel. 4772-5244
Parrilla / Argentine barbecue

La Furchina
Paraguay 3839 tel. 4776-2835
Cocina Italiana / Italian cuisine

La Mamá Rosa
Jufré 202 tel. 4773-2913
Cocina Argentina / Argentine cuisine

La Placita
Jorge Luis Borges 1636
Tel. 4832-6444
Cocina Italiana / Italian cuisine

Las Violetas
Av. Scalabrini Ortiz 2680
Tel. 4832-3968 / 1392
Parrilla / Argentine barbecue

La Tranquera
Av. Figueroa Alcorta 6464
Tel. 4784-6119
Parrilla / Argentine barbecue

Lindo Jardín
Cabello 3419 Tel. 4802-6851
Cocina China / Chinese cuisine

Morizono
Paraguay 3521 Tel. 4823-4250
Cocina Japonesa / Japanese cuisine

Museo Renault
Av. Figueroa Alcorta 3301
Tel. 4802-9629
Cocina Japonesa / Japanese cuisine

Nacachi
Jorge Luis Borges 1627
Tel. 4833-3311
Minutas / Fast food

Octavio
Salguero 2743 Tel. 4806-0035
Pastas

Oviedo
Beruti 2602
Tel. 4822-5415 / 4821- 3711
Cocina Española / Spanish cuisine

Paper Moon
Cerviño 3732
Tel. 4805-4643
Cocina Francesa / french cuisine

Park Zoo
Av. Sarmiento 2725
Tel. 4806-1835
Internacional cocina / International cuisine

Eyewitness Travelguide to Buenos Aires

Pimienta
Paraguay 3512
Tel. 4824-7590
Cocina Argentina / Argentine cuisine

Pizza Cero
Cerviño 3701 Tel. 4803-3449
Pizzas

Pizza Donna
Av. Santa Fe 3202 Tel. 4822-4206
Pizzas

Plaka
Arévalo 2725 Tel. 4777-6051
Cocina Griega / Grek cuisine

Puerto Sol
Bulnes 2593 tel. 4802-8640
Cocina Argentina / Argentine cuisine

Provoletto
Huergo 190 tel. 4778- 3001
Parrilla / Argentine barbecue

Rincón Orgánico
Gurruchaga y Castillo
Tel. 4777-5082
Cocina Australiana / Australian cuisine

Rock Garden
Ugarteche 3154 tel. 4806-9178
Cocina Internacional / International cuisine

Romario
Cabello 3700 Tel. 4802-4732
Pizzas

Sahara
Cabrera 4223
Cocina Arabe / Arabian cuisine

Salguero y el Río
Av. Rafael Obligado y Salguero
Tel. 4801-5422
Minutas / Fast Food

Sarkis
Thames 1101
Tel. 4772-4911
Cocina Arabe / Arabian cuisine

Scuzi I
Cabello 3601 Tel. 4804-2900
Cocina Internacional / International cuisine

Sítara
La Pampa 735 tel. 4784-2160
Cocina Hindú-Pakistaní / Hindu-Pakistanese cuisine

Súbito
Salguero 2741 tel. 4806-0033
Pizza y Pasta

Tabaré
Charcas 3387 Telefax 4821-7598
Parrilla / Argentine barbecue

Tago Mago
Av. Rafael Obligado y Salguero
Tel. 4804-2444
Cocina Argentina / Argentine cuisine

Te Mataré Ramirez
Paraguay 4062
Tel. 4831-9156
Cocina Exótica / Exotic cuisine

The Horse
Av. Del Libertador 3880
Tel. 4773-4847
Cocina Internacional / International cuisine

Xalapa
El Salvador 4800 Tel. 4833-6102
Cocina Mexicana / Mexican cuisine

Yamani
Julián Alvarez 1939 Tel. 4862-2848
Cocina vegetariana / Vegetarian cuisine

Yasmin
Cabrera 4625 tel. 4832-5278
Cocina Libanesa / Lebanese cuisine

PUERTO MADERO

Agua Dulce
Av. Ing. Huergo 400 Tel. 4345-0900
Cocina internacional / International cuisine

Bahía Madero
Av. A. Moreau de Justo 292
Tel. 4319-8733
Pizzas

Bice
Av. A Moreau de Justo 192
Tel. 4315-6216
Cocina Italiana / Italian Cuisine

Divino Buenos Aires
Cecilia Grierson 28 tel. 4312-1221
Cocina internacional / Internationale cuisine

Dizzy Lizzy
Av. A Moreau de Justo 846
Cocina Estadounidense / American cuisine

Dock Café
Av. A Moreau de Justo 350/40
Tel. 4319-8719
Minutas / Fast Food

El Mirasol del Puerto
Av. A Moreau de Justo 202
Tel. 4315-6277
Cocina Argentina

Fechoría
Av. A Moreau de Justo 1140
Tel. 4342-8609/4949
Cocina Italiana / Italian cuisine

Hereford
Av. A Moreau de Justo 1140
Tel. 4319-8715
Parrilla / Argentine barbecue

Il Gatto Trattorías
Av. A Moreau de Justo 1192
Tel. 4345-6565/4949
Cocina Italiana / Italian cuisine

La Caballeriaza
Av. A Moreau de Justo 580
Tel. 4314-2648/50

La Casona de Roque
Av. A Moreau de Justo 256
Tel. 4315-6343
Cocine Italiana / Italian cuisine

La Parolaccia
Av. A Moreau de Justo 1052
Tel. 4343-1679/4742/1345
Cocina Brasilera / Brazilian cuisine

La Rosada
Av. A Moreau de Justo 1170
Tel. 4313-7200
Cocina Internacional / International cuisine

Liberpool Pub
Av. A Moreau de Justo 350
Tel. 4319-8723
Minutas / Fast food

Piperno
Av. A Moreau de Justo 1942
Tel. 4313-0600

Puerto Cristal
Av. A Moreau de Justo 1080
Tel. 4331-3309/3669
Pizza y Pasta

Puerto Sorrento
Av. A Moreau de Justo 410
Tel. 4319-8730
Cocina Internacional / International cuisine

Rodizio
Av. A Moreau de Justo 840
Tel. 4334-3646/3638
Cocina Internacional / International cuisine

Spell Café
Av. A Moreau de Justo 740
Tel. 4334-0512
Cocina Internacional / International cuisine

Spettus Steak House
Av. A Moreau de Justo 876
Tel. 4334-4210/4126
Cocina IBrasileral / Braziianl cuisine

Tocorro
Av. A Moreau de Justo 1050
Tel. 4342-6032
Cocina Cubana / Cuban cuisine

Xcaret
Av. A Moreau de Justo 164
Tel. 4315-6260/61
Cocina Internacional / International cuisine

RECOLETA

A la Maracosa
M.T. de Alvear 225
Cocina Italiana / Italian cuisine

A'Mamma Liberata
J.E.Uriburu 1755
Tel.4804-3638
Cocina Italiana / Italian cuisine

Armenoville
Av. Alvear 1879
Tel. 4804-1033
Cena Show / Dinner Show

Eyewitness Travelguide to Buenos Aires

Au Bec Fin
Vicente Lópéz 1827 Tel. 44801-6894
Cocina Francesa / French cuisine

Babieca
Av. Santa Fe 1898 Tel. 4813-4914
Pizzas

Bonifacio
Guido 1939 Tel. 4805-2336 / 3996
Cocina Arabe / Arabian cuisine

Burger King
Av. Santa Fe 1997 Tel. 4812-5891
Fast Food

Campos del Pilar. Buenos Aires Design
Av. Pueyrredón 2501 Tel. 4806-1111 int. 1276
Parrilla / Argentine barbecue

Caruso. Buenos Aires Design
Av. Pueyrredón 2501 Tel. 4806-3299
Cocina Italiana / Italian cuisine

Champs Ellysees. Buenos Aires Design
Av. Pueyrredón 2501 Tel. 4806-1111
Minutas / Fast food

Clark's Recoleta
Junín 1777 Tel. 4801-9502
Cocina Internacional / International cuisine

Como
Juncal 2019 Tel. 4806-9664 / 7954
Cocina Internacional / International cuisine

El Beso
Pacheco de Melo 2909
Cocina Exótica / Exotic cuisine

El Bodegón de Peña
Peña 2475 Tel. 4806-7536
Cocina Argentina / Argentine cuisine

El Living
M. T. de Alvear 1540 Tel. 4811-4730
Cocina Internacional / International cuisine

El Tranvía
Av. Santa Fe 2933 Tel. 4823-6347
Pizza y Pasta

Fellini
Paraná 1209 Tel. 4811-2222
Cocina Italiana / Italian cuisine

Hard Rock Café. Buenos Aires Design
Av. Pueyrredón 2501 Tel. 4807-7625
Cocina Estadounidense / American cuisine

Harper's Junín
Junín 1773 Tel. 4801-7140
Cocina Internacional / International cuisine

Hippopotamus
Junín 1787 Tel. 4801-1040
Cocina Internacional / International cuisine

La Barra
Av. Del Libertador 932 Tel. 4812-1745
Cocina Española / Spanish cuisine

La Biela
Av. Quintana 596 Tel. 4804-0449
Minutas / Fast food

La Mansión. Park Hyatt Hotel
Cerrito 1455 Tel. 4326-3610
Cocina Francesa / French cuisine

La Parolaccia
Riobamba 1046 Tel. 4812-1053
Cocina Italiana / Italian cuisine

Lola
R. M. Ortíz 1805 tel. 4804-3410
Cocina Internacional / International cuisine

Luckie's. Buenos Aires Desin
Av. Pueyrredón 2501 Tel. 4806-1111
Cocina Estadounidense / Americaqn cuisine

Mc Donald's
Av. Córdoba 2031 Tel. 4964-0625
Fast Food

Mora X
Vicente López 2152 Tel. 4803-0261 / 2646
Cocina Francesa / french cuisine

Munich del Pilar. Buenos Aires Design
Av. Pueyrredón 2501 Tel. 4806-1111 / 6910
Cocina Internacional / International cuisine

Open Plaza
Av. Del Libertador 1800 Tel. 4802-7501 / 03
Fast food

Pizza Banana
Ayacucho 1425 Tel. 4812-6321
Pizza y Pasta

Porto Bello
J. E. Uriburu 1629 Tel. 4806-4275
Cocina Argentina / Argentine cuisine

Rodizio
Av. Callao 1292 Tel. 4814-1776
Cocina Internacional / International cuisine

Romanaccio
Av. Callao 1021 Tel. 4811-9888
Pizza y Pasta

Sahara Continental
Junín 1733 Tel. 4801-7544
Cocina Internacional / International cuisine

Sensu
Posadas 1101 Tel. 4815-5161
Cocina Japonesa / Japanese cuisine

Teatriz
Riobamba 1220 Tel. 4811-1915
Cocina Internacional / International cuisine

The Kilkenny. Irish Pub
M. T. De Alvear 399 Tel. 4312-7291
Restaurante Irlandés y Continental

The Shamrock
Rodríguez Peña 1220 Tel. 4812-3584
Cocina Irlandesa / Irish cuisine

Tiro Loco
Vicente López y Azcuénaga
Cocina Mexicana / Mexican cuisine

Troyka
Juncal 1647 Tel. 4414-1009
Cocina Rusa / Russian cuisine

Wendy´s . Buenos Aires Design
Av. Pueyrredón 2501 Tel. 4806-1111
Fast Food

RETIRO • PLAZA SAN MARTIN

A Mi Manera
Av. Del Libertador 308
Cocina Italiana / Italian cuisine

Blue Oyster
M. T. De Alvear 399 Tel. 4312-9179
Pescados y Mariscos

Club del Retiro
Juncal 743 Tel. 4326-7869
Parrilla / Argentine Barbecue

Dixie Diner
Av. Del Libertador y C. Pellegrini Tel. 4322-3646
Cocina Estadounidense / American cuisine

Don Corleone Blues Bar
Reconquista 924 Tel. 4311-8802
Cocina Italiana / Italian cuisine

Druid Inn
Reconquista 1040 Tel. 4312-9844
Cocina Internacional / International cuisine

El Aljibe- Sheraton Hotel
San Martín 1225 Tel. 4318-9000
Cocina Internacional / International cuisine

Filo
San Martín 975 Tel. 4311-0312 / 1871
Pizzas

Frontera
Esmeralda 941 Tel. 4313-0013
Cocina Internacional / International cuisine

Galani. Marriot Plaza Hotel
Posadas 1086 Tel. 4326-1234
Cocina Italiana / Italian cuisine

Jan Toki
Posadas 1029 Tel. 4393-0332
Cocina Vasca / Basque cuicine

La Brasseire. Marriot Plaza Hotel
Florida 1005 Tel. 4318-3000
Cocina Internacional / International cuisine

La Chacra
Av. Córdoba 941 Tel. 4322-1419 / 2593
Parrilla / Argentine barbecue

La Payanca
Suipacha 1015 Tel. 4312-5209
Cocina Criolla / Native cuisine

Eyewitness Travelguide to Buenos Aires

La Querencia
Esmeralda 1392 Tel. 4393-3205 / 3202
Cocina Criolla / Native cuisine

La Terraza Anush. Lancaster Hotel
Av. Córdoba 405 Tel. 4311-3021
Cocina Argentina-Arabe / Argentine-Arabian cuisine

Las Nazarenas
Reconquista 1132 Tel. 4312-5559
Cocina Argentina / Argentine cuisine

Ligure
Juncal 855 Tel. 4393-0644
Cocina Internacional / International cuisine

Morizono
Paraguay y Reconquista
Tel. 4314-0924 / 4443
Cocina Japonesa / Japanese cuisine

Orleans. Aspen Towers Hotel
Paraguay 857 Tel. 4312-9172
Cocina Internacional / International cuisine

Piola
Libertad 1078 Tel. 4812-0690
Cocina Italiana / Italian cuisine

Plaza Mayor
Posadas 1052 Tel. 4393-5671
Cocina Española / Spanish cuisine

Romario
Montevideo 1655
Tel. 4814-5210
Pizzas

Sensu
San Martín 760
Tel. 4319-5103
Cocina Japonesa
Japanese cuisine

The Tower Lounge.
Sheraton Hotel
Av. Leandro N. Alem 1193
Tel. 4318-9000 int. 2510
Cocina Internacional / International cuisine

WHERE TO GO DANCING TANGO.
Club Almagro: *Medrano 522 - vier., sáb. y dom. de 23 a 3 hs.*
Club Helénico: *S. Ortiz 1331 - vie., sáb.y dom. de 23 a 3 hs.*
Cuartito Azul: *San Juan 2926 - vie., sáb y dom. desde las 21 hs.*
Boedo-Salón Bailable: *Boedo 722 - vi., sáb.dom.desde las 23 hs.*
La Escuela del Tango: *Ctes.3159 - lun., mie.y vie. de 18,20 a 23 hs.*
Viejo Correo: *Diaz Velez 4820 - todos los días desde 20 hs.*
Confitería Ideal: *Suipacha 384 - mar. a dom. desde 20 hs.*
Megafon: *Chacabuco 1072 - lun., mie., jue. y dom. desde 21 hs.*
Club Bohemio: *Necochea 948*
Sabor a Tango: *Belgrano 2448*
Glorias Argentina: *Bragado 6875*
Café Tortoni: *Av. de Mayo 825*
La Viruta: *Armenia 1366.*

TANGO SHOWS AND DANCE HALLS SOUTH OF THE CATHEDRAL AND IN SAN TELMO QUARTER
A Media Luz: *Chile 316* / **Casa Blanca:** *Balcarce 668*
El Viejo Almacén: *Balcarce esq. Independencia*
Niño Bien: *Humberto Primo 1462*
Bar Sur: *EE.UU. 299* / **El Querandí:** *Perú 602*
La Convención: *C.Calvo 375*
Megafón: *Chacabuco 1072*
La Trastienda: *Balcarce 460*
Moliere: *Chile 299*
La Ventana: *Balcarce 425*
Michelángelo: *Balcarce 433*
Taconeando: *Balcarce 411*

Mate

What we call mate is an infusion with a nice taste and drinking it with friends has becoma such a widespread tradition that we might say it is a national custom. The Guaraní tribes discovered the plant it is made up of, which is called yerba, and they also found that its leaves are good for people's health. The Jesuits later started to drink it as tea (in mate bags) and they created a system for growing the herb or plant (yerba paraguensi) that we use to make mate.

The way we make and drink this infusion is also taken from the Guaraní tribes, which proves how ingenious their culture used to be. The gourd (also called mate), the straw (which we use to zip the drink), the kettle and the yerba are the basic elements you need if you want to drink some good mate.

Mateas a word has two different meanings: on the one hand, it is the drink itself and, on the other hand, it is the gourd, which also has different names according to the size, namely: the big ones are called porongos and those that have flat sides are called galletas.

Even though all mates were made out of pumpkins at the beginning, nowadays almost any material is good enough to pour some yerba and water in it. Some of them have silver decorations and others are entirely made up of silver or China. The straw or bombilla is the means by which we zip the liquid. It has been a metal straw since the Jesuits' times, but the Guaraní tribes used to have cane straws.

Sharing your mate and bombilla is a token of good manners, fraternity and peace.
Mate as a drink may take several names according to the way you make it, namely:
Bitter mate or cimarrón: just plain hot water and yerba.
Sweet mate: hot water, yerba, and sugar (white or brown).
Tereré: cold mate. You may use either cold water or citric fruits' juice.
Milk mate: hot milk and yerba.
Mate with coffee: yerba and hot coffee.
Mate Cocido: served as tea either in teabags or boiling the yerba. You may add some milk.

Eyewitness Travelguide to Buenos Aires

"Mate" is a popular infusion in Argentina. It has a nice taste and sharing it with friends is a typical tradition in Buenos Aires.

**This book was printed in
january of 2000.**